A Modern

Photography for Beginners

Minolta Corporation
Ramsey, New Jersey

Doubleday & Company
Garden City, New York

Photo Credits: All the photographs in this book were taken by the editorial staff unless otherwise credited. Cover: A. Moldvay; p. 3: J. DiChello; p. 4: P. Bereswill

Minolta Corporation
Marketers to the Photographic Trade

Doubleday & Company, Inc.
Distributors to the Book Trade

This book and the other books in the Modern Photo Guide Series were created and produced by Avalon Communications, Inc. and The Photographic Book Co., Inc.

Library of Congress Catalog Card Number 81-71228
ISBN: 0-385-18139-6

Cover and Book Design: Richard Liu
Typesetting: Com Com (Haddon Craftsmen, Inc.)
Printing and Binding: W. A. Krueger Company
Paper: Warren Webflo
Separations: Spectragraphic, Inc.

Manufactured in the United States of America
10 9 8 7 6 5 4 3 2 1

Contents

Technique Tips

Throughout the book this symbol indicates material that supplements the text and which has been set off for your special attention. You can apply the data and information in these Technique Tips immediately to get better results in your photography.

Introduction

Excitement, love, fascination, and joy are your companions in photography, where intense creative possibilities blend with scientific precision. The art and craft of your work are simplified by modern cameras, automatic accessories, and high-speed films that capture your subjects even in low light.

This book will show you how to get the best possible results from these extraordinary photographic advancements, how to master the photographic techniques that will let you express exactly what you desire on film. No matter how automatic your 35mm single-lens reflex may be the creative expression of photographic ideas is still the most important part of photography. Even with automatic equipment you can often control the final results on film, tailoring the rendition to personal taste. Use the techniques shown in this book to refine your talent. The step-by-step instructions in this book will show you how.

Why do we enjoy photography? Some see it as a pleasurable way to remember loved ones or to create a record of exciting voyages. Teachers appreciate photography because photographs are powerful teaching tools; parents lovingly collect photographic records of children growing up; naturalists record the beauty and drama of nature's world; gardeners put flowers on film for a permanent garden of delights. What you want from photography is the important consideration.

How do you create photographs? Begin by seeing subjects from several points of view. Before you push the shutter release take time to decide on composition. How you arrange the subject in the viewfinder determines the impact of each image you record on film.

Creative photography involves controlling the variables of putting light on film. Here, the photographer used a filter to modify the color and exposure settings to control the amount of light striking the film to achieve an intriguing silhouette. Photo: T. Tracy.

Careful composition is often the difference between a snapshot and an image that captures mood and emotion. Take plenty of time to decide fundamental things such as camera angle and distance from the subject; the improved results will make it worth the effort. Photo: J. DiChello.

Creative Photography

The creative approach to making photos carries you beyond your equipment. Once you have mastered the details, you will be able to begin experimenting with your new-found artistic freedom, to be able to express through your photographs. Your personal interpretations of the world around you, be bold, be experimental, challenge your eyes to search. Look into, beyond, below, above—for to create is by definition to see something in a new way.

Can a snapshot be useful? A quickly taken snapshot, perhaps technically acceptable thanks to a modern automatic camera, can be a valid record of what was in front of the lens when you released the shutter. In some cases a snapshot—grabbed without consideration to angle, composition, lighting, or controlled focus—is better than no photo at all. But why not advance from the snapshooter approach to that of the creative photographer?

To do this, learn to take more care in seeing. Decide for yourself what angle and composition best capture the subject or express your feelings. Make the photographs instead of just taking them.

A modern 35mm single-lens reflex camera will make it easy to get the most from your photographic efforts, whether you want to take excellent snapshots or highly sophisticated, professional-looking pictures. The 35mm SLR is the most versatile and widely used type of camera today. Photo: B. Sastre.

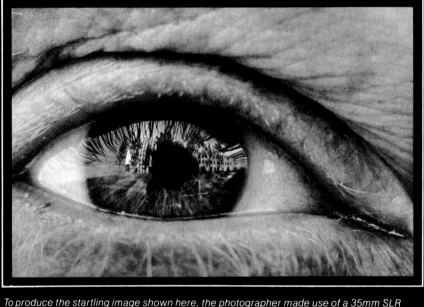

To produce the startling image shown here, the photographer made use of a 35mm SLR camera, a close focusing (macro) lens, and careful positioning so that a nearby building would be reflected in the eye. Note also the eerie effect of the reflected eyelashes. Photo: F. Leinwand.

Mastering Techniques

You can get maximum pleasure from photography by first mastering the techniques that will free you to create the kind of photographs you want or need. Your technically perfect photographs will be enriched by artistic composition, sensitive interpretation, appropriate display. Others will be happy to see your photos. Success begins with the choice of equipment. When you begin with a camera that is well suited to your style of photography, the techniques become clear, clean, understandable.

To get the fastest results with the techniques described in the following chapters we recommend a modern single-lens reflex camera. Most of the creative ideas and step-by-step instructions can be applied to other less sophisticated cameras, but the 35mm single-lens reflex is by far the most versatile and universally accepted camera for general use.

The single-lens reflex camera using 35mm film is so versatile that everyone from beginners to fashion photographers to astronauts use this design. Although the 35mm SLR is the most popular, it need not be expensive. A sturdy, modern model with built-in behind-the-lens meter, automatic exposure control, flash capability, and sharp lens can be purchased for the price of a few good dinners.

Techniques of focusing, composition, depth-of-field control, and use of different lenses are all simplified when you choose a single-lens reflex camera. Seeing your subjects directly through the taking lens lets the camera become a refined extension of your eye.

This book shows you how to achieve maximum success with your equipment. Now is the time to advance your technical understanding and heighten artistic sensitivity. Read on.

The 35mm SLR will allow you to see exactly what will be recorded on your film. This is a tremendous asset when you make pictures that depend on careful placement of objects in the field of view. Photo: P. Bereswill.

1

The Pleasures of Photography

Making photographs can be a great deal of fun. Looking at your photographs can bring pleasure to you and to all who see them. Certainly you enjoy photography if you are reading this book. Sharing your outstanding work will bring rewarding compliments, give pleasure to others and enrich your own life. Photographs remind us of friends and loved ones, help us appreciate life, and recall happy times.

There are any number of possible uses for photography, ranging from the creation of abstract, purely artistic images to the illustration of technical or scientific material. However, while the ways you use your images may vary, and while certain types of photography may require specialized equipment or techniques, certain elements are constant—for example, the knowledge of correct films for individual purposes, exposure, composition, lighting, depth-of-field control, and so forth. All of these will be discussed in this book. Whatever you choose to do with you photographs will be based upon your knowledge of these basic techniques.

Night photography is just one of the many exciting areas that is open to those with a knowledge of photography. To capture the special magic of a night scene you must understand the problems of long exposure and have a tripod and cable release at your disposal to execute the shot. Photo: T. Tracy.

Uses of Photography

Capture Life. Photography lets you capture forever important moments of life. By keeping your camera ready for meaningful events you will build a priceless record of what you love most. Browsing through a photographic album is a way of looking back over the past. It is a wonderful way to recall the happiest, most meaningful moments in your life.

With your camera, people and places visited around the world may be recorded forever, ready to bring years of pleasure when you are back home again. Taking travel photographs is easy and fun when you apply the techniques explained in later chapters. Modern cameras and film are so well matched that you will want to carry them everywhere. If you enjoy using instant film, consider taking photos of people in the countries you visit, then presenting the prints as on-the-spot gifts. This is a way to make friends quickly, and to overcome the language barrier too.

Photographs Help. Creating photographs will help you express feelings that cannot be put into words. The best photographers put emotion into their work. Asking a photographer to explain an artistic photograph is like asking a painter or sculptor to turn his art into words. If such a literal translation were possible the artist would use words to begin with. Documentary and educational photographs often are assisted by a few words or captions. But even these slice-of-life photographs can contain elements impossible to express effectively in words.

Photograph whatever you find beautiful or fascinating. The choices are unlimited because each of us sees the world from a personal point of view. Once you fully understand the mechanics of your camera, your taste will influence composition, angle, the time of day you choose to photograph subjects. When you first begin to apply the techniques explained in the following chapters you will do it with full awareness, but soon the procedures will become second nature, nearly automatic.

Photographs help identify. Your hobby is a natural resource for photographic subjects. The photographs will enrich your appreciation of any leisure activity, such as the collection of antiques, coins, crafts, or dolls. Sharp, close views help experts provide identification, evaluation, or a history of the subjects. Your photos protect the hobby collection by providing a record for insurance, and as reference to repair valuables.

Artistic Abstractions. Not all successful photographs include people or realistic images of the world. Some of the most dramatic compositions are of natural subjects turned into abstract designs by visually creative photographers. Photographing designs in nature is a never-ending challenge.

Some patterns to search for occur in man-made objects such as product packaging, parts of machines, buildings. Get in close, turn the straight view to an abstract pattern, help others to see things in a different light or from a new angle.

Technique Tip: Looking at Things in a New Way

To make your photographic seeing grow — especially as a beginner—take an extra picture or two in a new way, once you have photographed a subject in the way you originally planned.

Make the extra pictures as different as possible. Go to the opposite extreme. If you have been shooting close-up, move back to take in everything, or even to view the subject from a distance. If you have been exposing for full tonal range, try a silhouette. If you have been shooting for extremely realistic representation, try making the subject abstract.

Do not reject any impulse or idea, no matter how wild. You can't predict the visual effect of something different. Instead, try it—to *see* what will happen.

You'll have failures, of course. But you will also discover ways of looking at a subject, and ways of making images, that you couldn't have imagined.

Designs in nature are exciting. For example, tree trunks offer extraordinary possibilities for form, mass, pattern, texture, design, color. Water changes character with reflections, flow, or form such as ice, snow, fog, mist, and drizzle.

You might collect pictures of skies—sunrises, sunsets, moon phases, cloud patterns, reflections in water or glass; consider a collection of skies as reflected in sunglasses around the world or in different seasons.

Slides. Showing slides is easy, the best way of sharing pictures with several people at a time. It is easy to do with modern projectors. Once the slides are loaded into trays, they can be projected at a moment's notice. It is exciting to see your color images many times larger than life size. Imagine a rose or a happy face in full color, greatly enlarged, on your living-room wall or screen! Perhaps you would like to make photos of a hobby event, an antique boat show, a Little League game. The techniques explained in this book will enable you to make the kind of images fellow club members will be delighted to view. Sharp, well-composed slides are superior teaching tools, too. Perhaps you would like to create a sequence that will teach others how to do something such as build a model, make a garden, or use a camera.

Prints for Display. You may wish to display photographs of which you are especially proud. The print is the best means of doing this. Labs run by Kodak or smaller companies around the world make thousands of prints from slides and negatives each day. Your photographs will bring daily pleasure when they are displayed in albums, desk frames, and on the wall.

Depending on your aims, there is a camera to suit them. Most people find the versatile 35mm SLR and its many accessories readily adaptable for their needs. Photo: M. Fairchild.

Matching Equipment to Needs

How do you want to use photography? What are you interested in photographing and why? How will the photos be used? These are the questions to be answered before you can choose the best equipment for your work. Match the equipment to your desires.

If you only want color prints of family events, travel views, parties, and similar occasions, then a medium-priced, fully automatic, fixed-lens camera loaded with negative color film is the least complicated way to reach your goal. New models of these cameras have built-in electronic flash so you need to use only a single piece of equipment under all conditions. The ultimate in point-and-shoot cameras combines these easy-to-master features with fully automatic focusing. All you do is compose the photograph and push the shutter release. Perhaps even a pocket-size 110 camera will satisfy your needs, especially if you mainly want prints.

If you spend a lot of time on, or in, the water you might want to purchase one of the watertight rangefinder cameras designed for such purposes. The most sophisticated of these—and the most expensive—is the Nikonos, which offers interchangeable lenses and automatic light metering, and can be used at considerable depths. Less versatile and less expensive brands are also available.

Instant-print cameras are especially useful when you want to make an immediately available record of objects or events, for example to check certain elements of lighting or composition before making a final record on regular print or slide film. They are also excellent tools for introducing children to photography, as they gratify the child's need for immediate results.

However, you might want to photograph small objects as part of a hobby, perhaps stamps, coins, or crafts. The photographs will be used to create slide programs for club presentations. Perhaps a few photos will be used as insurance records, holiday greeting cards, or as prints for decorative display. Since you may want to photograph the subjects on black or white paper or a similar contrasting background, your camera must permit some manual control over exposure such as a film-speed (ISO/ASA) dial you can use to program the metering system, or manual setting capability to override an automatic exposure system. If maximum quality is required in photos of extremely small objects, your camera should permit the lens to be changed so you can photograph with a reversed lens, a lens on extension tubes or an accessory bellows, since without an interchangeable lens option you are limited to using add-on close-up lenses.

In contrast, if you are interested in capturing wildlife you must have a telephoto lens and fast shutter speeds. If you want to freeze action, as in sports photography, your camera should offer shutter speeds up to 1/2000 sec. A camera that can be fitted with an autowinder or motor drive is a great advantage for fast-moving events.

All of these purposes—and many others as well—can best be realized with a 35mm SLR camera. These are available in varying degrees of technical sophistication and versatility, and costs will vary accordingly.

The least expensive cameras offer limited shutter speeds and fixed lens design; they may lack depth-of-field preview features and accept fewer advanced accessories. In contrast, the most expensive models are usually highly versatile professional tools which accept many different lenses and accessories. They have changeable focusing screens, metering options, and full information display inside the viewfinder. They accept motor drives and have a full range of shutter speeds from several seconds up to 1/2000 sec. These advanced 35mm SLR cameras are well suited to photographers who must photograph everything, from microscope slides to elephants or racing cars. In between these extremes of cost and sophistication are the medium-priced 35mm SLR cameras so popular with advanced amateurs. A camera well suited to your needs is a bargain, sure to save you time and money as it brings you years of pleasure.

2

Camera Choices

Choosing the best camera for your uses is simplified when you first compare the basic features of various models and then consider more advanced options according to your specific needs. The features found on all modern cameras you might consider are:

Viewing system
Focusing system
Exposure system (shutter speeds and lens aperture)
Film advance

Although these basic features are found in most cameras, from quite simple models to very sophisticated designs, they are not equally controllable.

35mm cameras offer a bewildering array of features. Consider them, but reduce the problem of camera choice to the major practical considerations:

1. A single-lens reflex camera lets you focus at all distances with any lens that can be mounted on the camera. Choose it if you must have maximum versatility.
2. A rangefinder camera provides the brightest image for viewing, and the fastest focusing. Choose it if your need to shoot freely under low light conditions is more important than using a great variety of lenses.
3. If you want to use a zoom lens, you must be able to see exactly what you are getting. Choose a single-lens reflex camera.
4. A shutter-priority exposure system lets you select a speed you can be sure will produce sharp pictures. Choose it if you want to shoot action and sports, or want to hand-hold long focal-length lenses.

To choose the correct camera for you, consider various operating features in terms of the kind of pictures you want to take. Single-lens reflex viewing was essential to get this picture with a long focal-length lens. The circular images of out-of-focus highlights in this photo are the result of using a mirror- design telephoto lens. Photo: B. Krist.

Viewing Systems

Direct Viewfinders and Rangefinders. Viewing systems permit you to frame the photograph. Simple cameras often have small windows for direct viewing, with no connection to any focusing feature. This permits only approximate composition with no preview of precise coverage or depth of field (range of sharp focus) possible. More sophisticated direct viewfinders offer a focusing connection called a rangefinder. Although it cannot preview depth of field or take accurate close-up photographs of small objects, the rangefinder does permit precise focus.

Twin-Lens Reflex. Cameras with two lenses—one used to focus and compose the picture and a second lens actually takes the photograph—are called twin-lens reflex cameras. Like the rangefinder cameras, these TLR models offer easy viewing even under dim light, precise focusing, usually rugged construction, but still no depth-of-field preview or precise control of composition, especially at close range.

Viewing fast-paced action directly through the camera lens makes it possible to capture pictures like this. For sports photography, a single-lens reflex camera is the best choice.
Photo: B. Docktor.

Camera viewing systems. (Top) Single-lens reflex: A mirror prism arrangement shows you exactly what the camera lens sees. The mirror moves out of the way at the moment of exposure. (Center) Range/view-finder: Adjustable or fixed frames mark off the lens field of view, a rangefinder permits focusing sharply; however, the viewfinder optics do not match the camera lens. (Bottom) Twin-lens reflex: A fixed mirror reflects the view through a separate lens that matches the camera lens focal length. Both lenses move in unison for focusing.

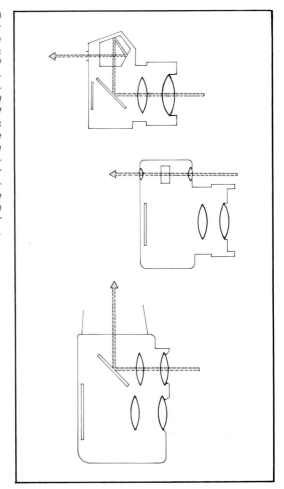

Single-Lens Reflex. The most precise viewing system by far is the single-lens reflex design. Single-lens reflex cameras have only one opening through which you view, focus, compose; you look through the same lens that actually takes the photograph.

Single-lens reflex cameras have a mirror behind the lens. The image of the subject is reflectd onto a viewing and focusing screen. In most 35mm SLR cameras, a prism in the viewfinder turns the image right way around so that you see the composition just as it appears in life. Without a prism the view is reversed left to right. At the instant the shutter is released the mirror lifts up, out of the way, so the image can strike the film. In most cameras the mirror automatically returns to the viewing system immediately after the shutter closes.

Since you are looking directly through the camera lens you can arrange precise composition, preview depth of field, and see the effect of filters, close-up lenses, and other lens attachments.

Exposure Systems

Shutter systems to let light strike the film range from a single simple lens shutter in inexpensive pocket cameras through electronically controlled focal-plane shutters found in many 35mm SLR cameras and some reflex cameras of larger size. Exposure of film is controlled by two camera features; the shutter speed (how long the film is exposed), and the lens aperture (how much light strikes the film).

Since the lens aperture and the shutter work together to control the film exposure, these features can be independently adjusted in more

For night photography, you need a camera that permits manually controlled exposures. Automatic exposure control systems are rarely able to handle such situations. Photo: J. Meyers/West Stock, Inc.

sophisticated cameras. For example, in popular 35mm SLRs the aperture is controlled by a diaphragm which has many different openings, continuously variable from a large opening (to let in maximum amount of light) down to a small opening (for minimum amount of light). Simple cameras may have only one or two openings, and perhaps only a single shutter speed.

Advanced cameras usually have shutters with a range of speeds from a fully controllable B ("bulb") setting that keeps the shutter open as long as the shutter release is held down, to 1/500, 1/1000, or 1/2000 sec. Commonly, the range covers: B, l sec., 1/2, 1/4, 1/8, 1/15, 1/30, 1/60, 1/125, 1/250, 1/500 sec. and so on, to the fastest speed.

Automatic Exposure Control Systems. Many advanced 35mm SLRs have built-in meters coupled to a semi- or fully automatic exposure control system. The meters are very sensitive and can operate at low light levels with a wide range of film sensitivities (ISO/ASA ratings). The two most popular automatic exposure systems are:

Aperture priority (aperture preferred)
Shutter priority (shutter preferred)

With aperture priority, you select the lens opening (f-stop) and the exposure control system automatically sets the required shutter speed. Most cameras have some provision for showing you if the shutter speed selected is slower than 1/60 sec. This is because many photographs show blur or unsharpness from camera movement when taken with a hand-held camera at a shutter speed below 1/60 sec. The aperture priority feature is very useful for photographers who want full control over depth of field.

Shutter-priority cameras permit you to set the shutter speed but leave the aperture control up to the automatic system. This sort of control is useful for situations where you might need full control over the shutter speed.

Meter Features. Cameras with built-in meters and exposure control features usually display the exposure data inside the finder. You can see the selected shutter speed and f-stop without removing your eye from the viewfinder. Metering systems that rely on the photographer to make the speed or f-stop adjustment have either a needle or light-emitting diodes (LEDs) to correct settings for each picture.

Built-in meters require small batteries that are inserted in a compartment in the camera. Some automatic cameras will not work if the batteries are worn out or missing. Other automatic cameras offer a limited range of shutter speeds when batteries are worn out. The aperture-preferred automatic feature is less versatile when batteries fail because the shutter speeds are controlled by the batteries. Cameras with battery-operated f-stops (apertures) retain more versatility when batteries fail because the shutter still works at all speeds. You can adjust the f-stop manually according to your judgment or information from a separate hand-held meter.

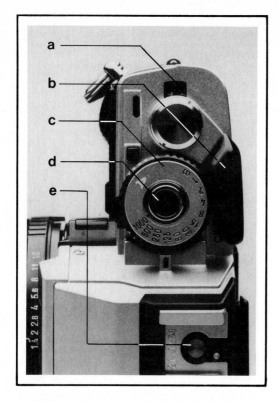

Here are some of the controls found on most 35mm SLR camera bodies:
a) frame counter
b) film advance lever
c) shutter speed dial
d) shutter release button
e) electronic flash synchronization contact/accessory shoe ("hot shoe").

Film Advance

Methods of advancing the film after each exposure range from simple winding knobs that bring each frame into place to motors that automatically advance the film after each exposure. The most common method is a thumb-operated lever located on the top right-hand end of most 35mm SLRs. The lever is stroked once (or sometimes several times) to advance the film and simultaneously to cock the shutter. It is designed to stop once the next frame is in place. Some cameras have an override that permits you to wind the shutter without advancing the film, thus giving you the option of making a double exposure (Chapter 9).

Features found on all but the simplest cameras, in addition to the basic features mentioned on page 18, are:

Frame Counter for the number of frames exposed (or remaining for use, in some models)
Connection to synchronize a flash unit with the shutter
Tripod Socket

If you want to make multiple-exposure images, look for a camera that lets you override the usual double-exposure prevention feature.
Photo: J. Sarapochiello.

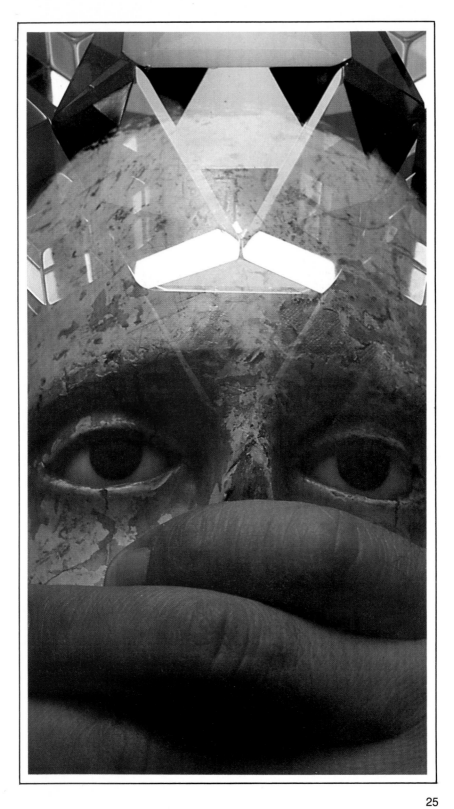

Pocket Types. These usually feature easy-to-load 110- or 126-size film cartridges which also set the camera exposure controls correctly according to the type of film in the cartridge. The 110 film format is often used in pocket cameras. Composition is done by simple direct viewing. Focusing may be fixed, or adjustable in broad steps, as indicated by symbols of one person, several people, and a mountain (close, medium, and distant focus). There are a few single-lens reflex 110-size cameras which offer direct through-the-lens focusing. A flash system may be built in.

Instant Film Cameras. Cameras that use self-processing instant film come in a variety of designs: single-lens reflex, with automatic film advance; very simple models with direct window viewing to provide general composition; rangefinder models that have built-in automatic metering systems; and models with combined automatic focusing and automatic exposure control. Many models accept attachments such as close-up lenses.

Medium- and Large-Format Cameras. Film sizes larger than 35mm are seldom required by hobby photographers. Many advanced and professional photographers do all of their work on 35mm film. Top quality color illustrated publications such as the National Geographic magazine get most of their photographs from 35mm color slides. However, large film formats have some advantages that apply to a few limited areas of photography. For example, when ultra-high-quality enlargements must be made or when a printing operation is not equipped with the most modern machines, a large negative or transparency is often preferred. When retouching is required, as in some portrait and fashion work, the larger film formats are preferred. When ultimate control of linear distortion and perspective is needed, as with some product photography and architectural subjects, a view camera with adjustable lens board and back will be used with a large film size.

Some professionals like the bright viewing and large focusing screen of twin-lens reflex cameras that take 2¼″ × 2¼″ pictures on 120-size film. More useful are single-lens reflex cameras that use 120 film for a variety of picture formats. Like their 35mm counterparts, these large-format SLR cameras offer precise focusing even at close range, exact composition, preview for depth of field, and sometimes behind-the-lens metering.

Single-lens reflex 2¼ × 2¼ models with interchangeable lenses and leaf shutters are favorites with fashion photographers. The shutter built into each lens permits electronic flash to be used at many shutter speeds, sometimes an advantage in illustrative or industrial photography.

Automatic 35mm Models. These automatic cameras are designed for photographers who want the convenience of fully automatic photography with the low cost and wide selection of 35mm film. Fully automatic 35mm cameras are available in rangefinder models, auto-focus models, and

Pictured here are three cameras, each designed with a different photographer in mind. The medium format, motorized SLR at left is primarily for professional, studio use. The small automatic 35mm rangefinder camera at center is best suited for quiet, unobtrusive snapshooting. The automatic exposure 35mm SLR at right is well suited to a variety of picture making situations, both amateur and professional.

single-lens reflex designs. The rangefinder types are lightweight, easy to carry, have fixed focus lenses, and sometimes offer built-in electronic flash. Often the models with a non-interchangeable lens have a slightly wider than normal angle of view so you can include many people in the frame, even in cramped quarters.

Advanced 35mm SLRs. The advanced 35mm single-lens reflex cameras offer the best of automatic features and photographer control. Many models permit you to use either automatic exposure control or manual control. All modern 35mm SLRs of advanced design have meters that read the light from behind the lens. Some models meter the light directly at the film plane, others at the focusing screen.

Advantages of the advanced 35mm SLRs include interchangeable lenses; synchronization with electronic flash; a full range of shutter speeds from very slow to very fast; numerous advanced accessories such as interchangeable prisms, finders, focusing screens, motor drives and film winders; and precise double exposure possibilities. Usually you have a choice of many lenses from the original manufacturer and from independent lensmakers as well.

Unusual camera angles or special lenses sometimes require the use of special viewfinder accessories. A waist-level finder and a focusing screen with a central split-image rangefinder make getting a shot like this much easier. Photo: J. Scheiber.

Choosing an Advanced 35mm SLR

After considering all of the camera choices, from tiny, pocket-size models using 110 film up to professional view cameras with expensive sheet film and unwieldy bulk, most beginners choose a 35mm single-lens reflex camera. Among the many brands costing nearly the same you will find some more suitable for your style of photography than others.

Viewing/Focusing. Some finders offer a choice of many focusing screens. Here are some points to consider in making your selection: Is the information display bright enough? Can you see the whole picture area? Do you want a model that offers interchangeable diopter inserts so you can use the camera without your glasses, if you normally wear them? Does the camera offer a waist-level finder or a right-angle finder that screws into the prism for low-angle viewing? Can you focus easily with the type of focusing glass available?

Shutter Speeds. Does the range go slow enough and fast enough for your uses? How easy is it to change speeds? Can you use the shutter when batteries are worn out or not in the camera? Is the shutter and mirror combination quiet enough for your anticipated use?

Metering and Automatic Features. Does the built-in meter cover the sensitivity (ISO/ASA) range you need? Is the meter easy to read and to set? Will the metering system work with the lenses you plan to use? How many batteries are needed for the camera to work fully? How long do the batteries last? Can you replace the required batteries easily? Does the camera offer automatic exposure control? Several advanced 35mm SLRs do not. If so, can you adjust exposure manually, or are you forced to accept what the automatic controls do? Is the meter easily adjustable for intentional over- or underexposure, and if so by how many stops? Does the camera offer a choice of shutter-priority or aperture-priority automatic exposure features, or only one or the other?

Flash Capability. Does the shutter synchronize with electronic flash at the speeds you need? Does the manufacturer offer special dedicated flash units that offer additional convenience in some applications? Is there a hot shoe socket, and if so is it conveniently located?

Lens Selection and Attachments. Are the lenses you plan to use available for the model under consideration? What lenses are offered by the camera manufacturer? By other independent manufacturers? How does the lens attach to the camera—by screw mount (rather slow to use) or fast-action bayonet? Do the available lenses take the same size filters and accessories, or is each lens different? It is both convenient and a money-saving feature to have a common accessory/filter size for all or most of your lenses. How easily do the lenses focus and which way does the focus control turn? Some brands turn left to right for close focusing, others go the opposite direction. It is wise to have all lenses focus the same way, especially if you work with fast-moving subjects.

Overall Considerations. Does the camera body design fit your hands? Does the weight seem reasonable? Some brands offer lightweight, medium-weight, and heavy models. Are the strap lugs or attachment sockets sturdy and conveniently located? Is the camera well finished, appealing to your taste? Is factory service easily available in most areas where you will be using the camera? What accessories do you plan on using and are they easily available for the camera you are considering? Consider the international reputation of the manufacturer. Select a brand with a record of reliable service from a company with an excellent reputation.

3

Lens Selection

A single-lens reflex camera offers the chance to use a wide range of techniques because it can accept an almost unlimited variety of lenses. But this versatility makes the choice of appropriate lenses an important matter. In photography the camera lens becomes your eye on the world.

How Lenses Work. Your eye has an iris that automatically (involuntarily, in fact) closes to a small aperture in bright light, or opens wide when the light is dim. A camera lens is fitted with a diaphragm that works like our eye's iris, but often over a wider range or apertures, indicated by *f*-number settings (*f*-stop).

Your eye can focus near or far, but with essentially the same angle of view. Camera lenses are made in many different focal lengths, each showing a different angle of view. Without moving, a camera set in a stationary position can be made to see a wide view, medium view, or bring a distant object closer, simply by changing the lens.

Essentially, the lens performs four functions: 1. It defines a field of view; 2. It provides a sharp image of the subject; 3. It magnifies or reduces the subject size in the image; 4. It controls the amount of light passing to the film.

Changing the camera lens alters the image size of whatever subject the lens is focused on. For example, attach the camera to a tripod and focus on a subject about 3 meters (10 ft.) away. With a normal (50 to 55mm focal length) lens on a 35mm camera, you will see the subject plus an area around the subject. Now look at the subject through a 200mm lens from the same distance. The subject will be much larger in the frame—in fact four times larger—because the telephoto lens has magnified the image. Note that the angle of view has gone from moderate in the 50mm view to narrow with the 200mm telephoto lens.

A long telephoto lens is ideal for getting a close-up image of your subject when photographing from a distance. Photo: B. Sastre.

The normal 50mm lens offers a great deal of picture-taking versatility. Its close approximation of the way the eye views the subject makes it suitable for a wide variety of photographic situations. Photo: C. Child.

Normal Lenses

The normal 50mm lens that is often purchased with 35mm single-lens reflex cameras is a versatile, compact design, usually made with at least an f/2 maximum aperture for bright focusing on the ground glass. A maximum aperture of f/2 or f/1.2, permits you to use the lens under dim light conditions while still selecting a moderate shutter speed.

Normal lenses have an angle of view appropriate to the most popular subjects such as landscapes, small groups of people, several people doing something, moderately close portraits of one to three people, travel photographs. The perspective shown by a 50 to 55mm lens on a 35mm SLR offers a familiar undistorted image that seems correct. Only when a normal lens is focused at the closest distance in its range (30.5–61cm [1–2 ft.] on most models) will objects nearest the lens seem too large. For this reason the normal lens is not popular for close portraits of a single person. Whatever is closest to the lens—nose, forehead, or chin—often looks abnormally large. With flat subjects or those in which distortion is not important, close-ups can be made with inexpensive close-up attachments that permit normal lenses to focus closer than the usual 1 or 2 feet.

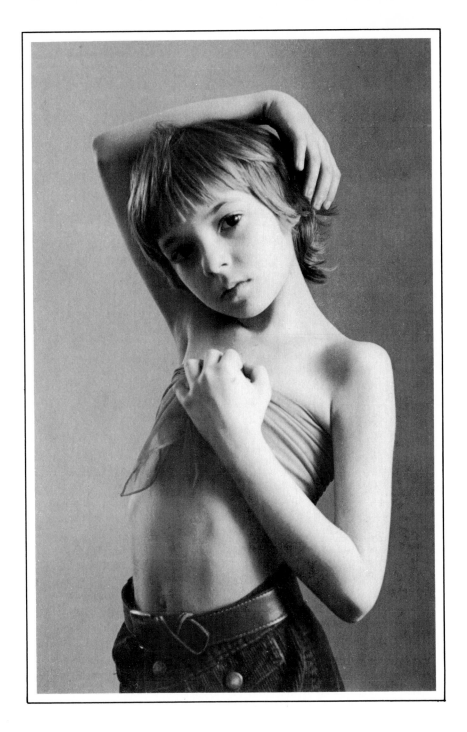

At four to five feet, a normal (50-55mm) lens will give you excellent half-figure or longer portraits. Working closer with this kind of lens for a portrait—for example, to get a head-and-shoulders shot—may produce some distortion of your subject's features. However, many other kinds of subjects are quite suitable for close-range pictures with a normal focal-length lens. Photo: N. deGregory.

Wide-Angle Lenses

Wide-angle lenses are exciting creative tools in the hands of an experienced photographer. A moderate wide-angle design, perhaps 28 or 35mm on a 35mm SLR, is adequate for many applications.

Moderate Wide-Angle Lenses. Groups of people indoors often can be included easily with a 35mm lens. Since these lenses are popular, you have a wide choice of models and prices; they usually have maximum apertures of at least $f/3.5$, with many offering $f/2.8$ or more. Although the 35mm is a moderately wide-angle lens, it can still create exaggerated perspective, useful in emphasizing some part of the subject. For example, a 35mm lens used from slightly above will make a person seem shorter. Photograph someone from ground level with a 35mm lens and the subject will seem taller, perhaps more powerful or glamourous than usual.

Ultra-Wide-Angle Lenses. Wider lenses, such as 28mm or 20mm, are more popular with advanced photographers. A 28mm lens is very useful in documentary and news photography where you may have to photograph several people in small quarters, without having freedom to move around or get farther away. The 20mm lens on a 35mm camera has an even wider view, but it tends to distort subjects, especially those toward the edge of the picture. For most general applications the 28mm wide-

Wide-angle lenses let you take in large landscapes. A 28mm or 35mm on your 35mm SLR will let you handle most wide-angle applications without a great deal of concern over the perspective distortion that can be so tricky with wider-angle optics. Photo: R. Holle.

Fisheye lens images that fill the frame show maximum curvature of subject matter close to the picture edges. When well composed, such images can dramatize a subject without calling undue attention to the type of lens used. Photo: B. Krist.

angle is a wise choice, with the 35mm being slightly restrictive, and the 20mm wider than you need under average conditions.

Fisheye Lenses. Fisheye lenses begin at 16mm for 35mm cameras, and go to 6mm in some models. These are specialized lenses seldom required by professionals but appropriate in some cases. Examples of such applications are for photographing in big pipes or tunnels, inside very small rooms where all doors and features must show, or outside to show the full sky and horizons.

Sometimes the fisheye perspective is used to dramatize a subject. Certainly the circular image of many fisheyes gives an unusual appearance and can be an excellent effect in slide programs or published features. A few fisheye lenses produce images which fill the rectangular film, but most of them create a circular image directly in the center of each slide or negative. Some designs have built-in filter wheels for exposure control. The least expensive fisheye lenses are actually accessory lenses that screw in front of other camera lenses to offer a 180-degree view. This sort of attachment is a better investment if you only plan on using a fisheye effect a few times each year. A prime fisheye lens for a 35mm camera usually costs more than the camera body, while the fisheye screw-in accessory can be bought for the price of a few good filters.

Long telephoto lenses (200mm and longer) will allow you to fill your 35mm frame with the intensity of sporting events from an unobtrusive distance. A fast shutter speed and steady camera are essential for this type of photograph. Photo: J. Peppler.

Telephoto Lenses

Making distant subjects larger in the picture is the job of the telephoto lens. To photograph small birds, distant landscape features, many sports, dangerous events, far away buildings, or to capture people candidly the telephoto lens is a necessity. Without the magnifying power of a telephoto lens the subjects would remain very small on the negative or slide. Even when photographs can be cropped and enlarged, it is better to capture the image as you wish, filling the frame with important material. The telephoto lenses can do this for you.

Moderate Telephoto Lenses. Portraits of people are especially attractive when taken with a moderate telephoto lens, 90 to 135mm on a 35mm camera. Such moderate telephoto lenses also permit you to photograph from several feet away while still filling the frame with a close view. This leaves room for reflectors or lighting equipment, and also makes the subject more comfortable. Perspective from the moderate telephoto lens is so pleasant that some photographers consider a 100 or 105mm lens as their "normal" lens.

Long Telephoto Lenses. Longer telephoto lenses, such as the 200 to 400mm types, are helpful with sports. Even professional photographers seldom can get close enough to sports action to fill the frame without the use of a telephoto lens. In many situations you are not allowed to get close, even if it is safe, so your best solution is to use a long telephoto lens. A 200mm telephoto is adequate for sports and some nature photography of large animals.

This lens is also long enough to give the compressing effect sometimes desired for artistic control. For example, if you photograph a group of people in a park with a fountain in the distance, using a telephoto lens, the people and fountain will seem much closer to each other than they are in life. Traffic jams look impossibly congested, as do crowds, when photographed with long telephoto lenses. Since telephoto lenses enlarge the subject, you are more likely to see camera shake or subject movement in photographs taken at medium shutter speeds. The solution is to use a tripod or a fast shutter speed—preferably both whenever possible.

The newer telephoto lenses are shorter and often lighter in weight than older models. Computer technology and recent improvements in optical glass have helped lens makers produce better lenses at relatively low cost. When considering a telephoto lens, check that the focal length is appropriate for your work. In 35mm photography the 100 to 135mm focal lengths are excellent for people portraits and studies of large birds that are tame or at least caged. If you wish to photograph small wildlife, a 300 to 400mm lens or longer is needed.

Lens Extenders (Tele-Converters)

One inexpensive way to get a telephoto effect is to put a lens extender between your camera body and lens. Popular extenders multiply the lens focal length by 1.5× to 3×, but they also change the f-stop ratings. See the table for data on these factors. A major advantage of using an extender is that the closest focusing distance does not change when a lens is combined with an extender. If your 50mm lens normally focuses to 1½ feet, with a 2× extender it becomes a 100mm telephoto lens that focuses to 1½ feet.

Extenders are far less expensive than individual lenses and they can be used with every lens you own. So, you can effectively double the number of lenses you have just by buying one extender. For best image sharpness, use an aperture of f/5.6 or smaller (and compensate exposure as required). Use the same precautions to avoid camera movement as you would with a telephoto lens: a fast speed, and a tripod if at all possible.

Lens extenders work with all lenses, but they are optically best suited for use with a telephoto lens. A 2X extender plus a 600mm lens provided a 1200mm focal length for this moon and tree picture. Close the lens two or three f-stops from the maximum aperture for optimum sharpness with an extender. Photo: M. Fairchild.

Lens extenders provide an inexpensive and extremely portable means to double or triple the focal length of your normal or telephoto lenses.

USING LENS EXTENDERS

Focal Length

New FL = Lens FL × Extender factor

Examples:

	1.5×	2×	3×
50mm lens + Extender:	1.5×	2 ×	3×
New Focal length:	75mm	100mm	150mm

Exposure

(A) *Through-the-lens* meter readings are accurate; expose as indicated.

(B) For readings *not taken through the lens,* reset ISO/ASA film speed on meter as shown, take reading, expose as indicated.

	1.5×	2×	3×
Extender:	1.5×	2×	3×
Divide ISO/ASA by:	2	4	8

(C) Instead of (B) above, use meter set at normal film speed and adjust indicated exposure:

	1.5×	2×	3×
Extender:	1.5×	2×	3×
Multiply shutter speed by:	2	4	8

or

	1.5×	2×	3×
Open aperture this many *f*-stops:	1	2	3

Zoom Lenses

A zoom lens has a variable focal length but maintains focus as you change from one focal length to another. Similar lenses, called varifocal or parfocal lenses, also can change focal length, but you must refocus every time. Modern zoom lenses are sharp, have moderate maximum f-stops of $f/3.5$ to $f/4.5$ and offer great convenience in providing precise composition. Thanks to advances in lens design the new zooms produce excellent image quality. For most photography you cannot notice any difference between pictures taken with top-quality zooms and those taken with fixed-focal-length lenses.

Having a single lens that contains a range of angles and magnifications is useful for travel, documentary, and sports photography. Some fashion photographers also like zooms because they can vary image size quickly without changing the distance between camera and model. Zoom lenses are available which cover all the general focal lengths, from wide-angle to telephoto. The least expensive types have moderate range of about $2\times$. This means the lens zooms to twice its shortest focal length. The most expensive and also the largest zoom lenses have an extensive range. For example, one model goes from 50mm normal to 300 mm telephoto, a good range for wildlife or sports work.

Zooming during an exposure can give your image a sense of motion. Put your camera on a tripod and try zooming during exposures of 1/8 sec. to 1 second. Photo: W. Holmes.

Most popular are the moderately wide to medium telephoto zooms, 35–70mm or 35–100mm for example. Zoom lenses are offered by camera manufacturers and by many international lens makers in mounts to fit all popular 35mm single-lens reflex cameras. A few zooms are available for 110 cameras and 2¼ × 2¼ SLRs.

Zoom Controls. Two different designs are used in zoom lenses for focus and zoom actions. Some lenses have a single moving ring to control the zoom action and focus. You push or pull to zoom, and turn side to side to focus, just as with a conventional lens. These are called one-touch zooms and are favorites with photographers who must work fast. The second design offers two separate control rings: one for the zoom action and another for focus. This two-touch design is an advantage if you wish to zoom during slow exposures. Since the zoom control is separate from the focus adjustment, you have no chance of twisting slightly out of focus during the zooming action.

Close Focusing. Some zoom lenses in the most popular ranges, with maximum focal length of about 70 to 210mm, offer a close-focusing feature, sometimes called macro-focusing. These zoom lenses permit you to focus closer than the 91 to 183cm (3–6ft.) common with telephoto lenses. Many permit subjects to be pictured at one-third to one-half life size on film. A few actually offer a life-size (1:1) image magnification when fitted with a matched tele-extender (sometimes called multiplier or converter) offered by the lens maker. Which close-focusing feature you need depends on the size of the smallest subjects you want to photograph.

If you want to fill the frame with small (5–7.6cm [2–3in.]) flowers, then a zoom lens that permits life-size or 1:1 magnification is useful. For usual portraits of people and moderate close-ups, a lens offering one-quarter to one-third life-size images is suitable.

Zoom Effects. The most useful effect of a zoom lens is its fast adjustment of focal length. With a single control you can choose an entire range of focal lengths, plus all the intermediate positions not even offered in single lenses. For example, you can zoom to 138mm on a 70 to 200mm zoom, if that is the magnification you want. Because zoom lenses permit such precise cropping in the camera, they are excellent for creating color slides: you want the whole frame to include only important matter because you can't re-crop at a later stage. For color prints and black-and-white photography, where cropping is so easily done in the darkroom as prints are made, the zoom may not be so necessary, but zooms remain a useful aid in filling the negative for maximum impact.

The actual zooming action is an effect that can be seen with slow exposures. To get a blur of color with streaks from highlights, put the camera with a zoom lens on a sturdy tripod. Take several photographs at the slowest shutter speeds, from 1 sec. to 1/8 sec., zooming the lens in or out as each exposure is being made. Another interesting effect that is easy to obtain with a zoom is to take two or three exposures on the same frame, each at a different focal length. These effects are most powerful when the camera is stationary, on a tripod.

Precise focusing is critical in close-ups because details are so large and the zone of sharpness is very shallow. Stopping the lens down for greater depth leads to long exposures, so use a tripod whenever possible. Photo: W. Updike.

Macro-Focusing Lenses

A macro-focusing lens is designed to focus very close, usually to produce images at least one-half life-size, often to full life-size or 1:1. (A normal 50mm lens for a 35mm camera focuses to about 51cm (20 in.), which produces an image only one-ninth life-size.) A life-size image is one in which your subject is the same size on the film as it is in life. For example, you can fill a 35mm color slide with a human eye or a small marigold. Since the macro-focusing lens is made for close focusing, it is also engineered to deliver maximum sharpness at close distances. A 55mm macro lens on a 35mm SLR has long been a favorite for copying documents, paintings, stamps, coins, and for photographing medium-sized flowers.

Some photographers prefer a longer macro, such as a 90mm, a 105mm, or even a 200mm macro. The longer focal lengths permit you to stay farther away from the subject while still getting a large image on film. Greater distance between subject and lens leaves room for lights, reflectors, or other devices.

Macro-focusing lenses can be used as standard everyday lenses too. The normal focal length (50–55mm) macro lenses do not have ultra-wide maximum apertures, since they are designed for maximum image quality rather than to let in lots of light. Some macros open to $f/2.8$, which is wide enough for most situations; but few photographers use the largest apertures with any frequency, because they need the depth of field delivered by small iris openings. (Depth of field is the near-to-far range in which details in the final image appear sharp. It increases as the f-stop is made smaller.)

A 200mm macro-focusing lens is ideal for close-ups of skittish subjects because it lets you work at increased camera-to-subject distances. The extra long focal length limits depth of field, so make sure to use a small aperture in order to render your subject sharply. Photo: J. Scheiber.

Perspective Control Lenses

If you enjoy photographing buildings or tall trees but do not like the tilted-back look that appears when you aim your camera up at a subject, consider using a perspective control or "tilt-shift" lens.

The perspective control lens, available in wide angle focal lengths of 28mm or 35mm, have shifting elements and a rotation knob. The lens can move up, down, or to either side; these movements can also be done at tangents, since the lens rotates in a full circle. Because the lens itself shifts, tall objects can usually be included in the frame without tilting the camera. Perspective control lenses have manual diaphragms: the diaphragm is opened to maximum aperture to focus and compose, then stopped down to take the photograph. These lenses are also useful for photographing around an object that cannot be eliminated from the picture by changing the camera angle: for example, if you must take a photograph from a fixed position but a window frame or post appears at one side of the image, you can eliminate the obstacle by shifting the lens.

If you tilt the camera upward to photograph a building or other tall structures, vertical lines converge to give the impression that it is falling over backwards. Photo: J. Scheiber.

Correct perspective is maintained when the camera back is vertical, but this takes in too much foreground. Photo: J. Scheiber.

Shifting the front element of a perspective-control lens upward adjusts the coverage to take in the building without having to tilt the camera. Photo: J. Scheiber.

General Considerations

Choose lenses with apertures useful in your work. The chart on the facing page will give you a good idea of what kinds of lenses are best for what subjects.

The lens you choose should accept the size filters and other accessories you have. It is an advantage to have your usual lenses (i.e., wide-angle, normal, moderate telephoto) with the same screw-in accessory size so all attachments are quickly interchangeable without adapter rings.

The lens should have an automatic diaphragm. Most lenses for SLR cameras do, so you can view and focus with the brightest image. Only special purpose lenses, such as the perspective control lens, must have manual diaphragms. For maximum convenience, select general-purpose lenses with automatic diaphragms.

If the lens does not come with a shade and/or a lens cap, these items should be easily obtainable. You should also be able to handle the lens easily—you may find some lenses too small, heavy, long, or short. For all lenses, get a skylight filter to protect the front element.

LENS FEATURE CHECKLIST

Purpose	Lens	Remarks
People portraits & candids	85 to 135mm	105mm is a favorite. Large maximum apertures ($f/2.5$) available.
Groups indoors, rooms, interiors	20 to 35mm	28mm is a good medium-wide-angle lens.
Small objects must fill the frame	55mm macro	Good for flat copy work (stamps, paintings)
	105mm macro	Useful when subjects cannot be approached closely; space needed between lens and subject for lights or reflectors.
	200mm macro	Dangerous subjects (wild animals); versatility for photographing far-away or very small subjects close-up
Distant objects must seem closer	200 to 400mm telephoto	Use with tripod when possible; slowest hand-held shutter speed: 1/250 sec.
Versatility	80–200mm zoom	Best for sports
	50–150mm close-focusing (macro) zoom	Best for general nature & travel because of compact design
	35–70mm zoom	Good for indoor people photos or documentary work in limited space
Architecture	35 to 28mm PC	Shift control preserves parallels.
Family activities; low-light	50mm	Wide apertures ($f/2$ to $f/1.4$) good for low light with fast shutter speeds for hand-held work; normal perspective.

◄Make sure an additional lens is suitable for the work you want to do and is convenient to use. Ideally, its aperture and focusing rings should turn in the same direction as your other lenses, and it should accept the same size accessories. Photo: R. Moore

4

Film Choice

Choosing the right film is just as important as having the appropriate equipment for each situation. With the best film for each occasion you will get superior results from your equipment. What are the basic types of film available for modern cameras? Besides the obvious choice between *color* or *black-and-white* you also must choose between reversal film for slides (transparencies) or negative film for prints.

Color film names that end with "-chrome" are designed to deliver slides; those that end in "-color" are processed to yield negatives from which prints are made. There is no similar distinction in black-and-white film names because virtually all are negative films.

You are not limited to just one kind of image with either type of film. You can get slides made from color negatives, prints made directly from slides, black-and-white prints from color or black-and-white negatives, and color negatives made from slides. Which possibility to choose depends on how you will use the photographs, what gives you the most pleasure.

Whether color or black-and-white, films have certain basic characteristics which determine the quality of the images they can produce. The major characteristics are: speed; graininess; contrast; color values, related to the set of dyes used in a particular color film; and resolving power, or the ability to record fine details distinctly. These are inherent, or built-in characteristics; we can take advantage of them simply by selecting a film that has the combination of characteristics we need to take a desired kind of picture.

To avoid the appearance of graininess, especially in middle-toned areas of your subject, choose a slow, fine-grained film. Photo: H. Weber.

Instant print cameras are ideal for quick shots that everyone wants to see right away. Photo: D. Dean.

Instant-Print Films

Polaroid Corporation and Eastman Kodak Company both offer various types of instant-print film. Instant-print film is relatively expensive compared to unprocessed 35mm film in magazines, but if you want prints, the cost differential between 35mm film with print processing and the instant print right from your camera is minimal. The obvious advantage of instant film is the rapidity with which you can judge the final photograph. If anything has gone wrong you can always take another photo right away.

Instant-print photography is excellent for such things as family snapshooting, parties, and situations where people want to share the pleasure of seeing the picture right away. The drawbacks are related primarily to the equipment. You must use a specially designed camera which is larger, heavier, and less versatile than a 35mm SLR camera. It takes fewer pictures from a single loading, and does not offer the advantage of interchangeable or zoom lenses. Also, you are limited to one print, in only one size, of each picture unless you are willing to pay for a somewhat involved copying process.

If you do want more copies, you must send the print to the manufacturer for duplicates, enlargements, or slides. Polaroid and Kodak offer this service to users of their instant-print films. Kodak labs accept this work through neighborhood dealers while Polaroid offers the service through the mail.

Most instant-print cameras are intended primarily for taking snapshots, but you can get good results with them. If you missed a shot for any reason you'll know it right away. Photo: J. Schafer.

Film Speed

Each type of film has a specific recommended speed or rating, expressed by a number. For years this number was called ASA (for American Standards Association) speed. Now the designation ASA is being changed to ISO (International Standards Organization) but the film rating numbers remain the same. Thus an ASA 400 film is also an ISO 400 film.

Film speeds refer to the relative sensitivity of each film type to light. Films with low sensitivity to light have low speed numbers and are called *slow* films. These include black-and-white films with ratings of ISO/ASA 32 to 50, and color films such as Kodachrome 25 (ISO/ASA 25). Medium-speed black-and-white films have ratings of about 100 to 200. In color, medium-speed films include the ISO/ASA 100 color negative types, Kodachrome 64, and Kodak Ektachrome 64 (ISO/ASA 64).

A fast film in black-and-white has a rating of at least 400, as with Kodak Tri-X. Highly sensitive color films are the 400 types such as Kodacolor 400, Ektachrome 400 and 200, and Ektachrome 160 tungsten. By special arrangement with the developing lab, some of these fast films can be processed for even higher ratings, which allow them to be used under even lower light levels.

ISO/ASA numbers are set up so that the number doubles as sensitivity to light doubles. As ISO/ASA 200 film is twice as fast as an ISO/ASA 100 film, four times as fast as an ISO/ASA 50 film, and half as fast as an ISO/ASA 400 film.

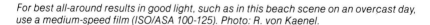

For best all-around results in good light, such as in this beach scene on an overcast day, use a medium-speed film (ISO/ASA 100-125). Photo: R. von Kaenel.

ISO FILM SPEEDS

4/7°	125/22°
5/8°	160/23°
• 6/9°	• 200/24°
8/10°	250/25°
10/11°	320/26°
• 12/12°	• 400/27°
16/13°	500/28°
20/14°	650/29°
• 25/15°	• 800/30°
32/16°	1000/31°
40/17°	1250/32°
• 50/18°	•1600/33°
64/19°	2000/34°
80/20°	2500/35°
•100/21°	•3200/36°

The left-hand speed of each pair is an arithmetic number; use it to set the ISO/ASA dial on meters. The right hand speed, marked °, is an equivalent logarithmic rating; use it to set the DIN (a European system) dial found on some meters.

Film speed doubles as the arithmetic numbers double, and as the logarithmic numbers increase by 3.

Meter dials may show only the numbers indicated by •; the in-between numbers are often shown by index marks. They are equivalent to ⅓-step changes in exposure. Not all meter dials include the highest and lowest speeds listed here.

In all cases choose the slowest, least sensitive film that will do the job. Slow films have fine grain and the most true-to-life colors. As film sensitivity increases the pattern grain becomes larger and colors are shown with less precision. For example, Kodachrome 25 is the best color slide film in terms of color rendition and a grainless look. It is a fine choice for bright situations, and where electronic flash provides strong illumination sufficient for the *f*-stops you want to use. If light is less bright or if you need very small *f*-stops (for great depth of field), a medium-speed film such as Kodachrome 64 or a faster film such as Ektachrome 200 would be better.

With black-and-white films the same rules apply. Choose the slowest film possible for the job. When you have the adequate light or the freedom to make long exposures without the camera or subject moving, Kodak Panatomic-X with a slow ISO/ASA of 32 is a good choice. Because the grain pattern of this film is extremely fine, even a small portion of the negative can be enlarged without showing too much grain.

For natural-looking photographs in dim light conditions, use fast films—those with an ISO/ASA speed of 400 or higher. The more noticeable graininess of these films often will enhance the mood of the scene. Photo: N. deGregory.

Grain and Contrast

Grain. Some general characteristics are common to all films, both color and black-and-white. The distribution of silver grains in a film may produce a visible pattern in the final image especially in light areas when big enlargements are made. This pattern is called graininess. Fast films have a more noticeable grain pattern (larger grain) than slow films. As a general rule, to get top quality prints and slides, use the slowest film suitable for the lighting conditions.

Sometimes a photographer will deliberately use a fast film to produce a grain pattern in enlargements, for a specific artistic reason. You must decide if the grain pattern from a specific film is suited to your taste or not. If you want only the subject to show, with no overlying pattern of grain, always choose slow film when you have adequate light. Fill the frame so that you use as much of the film area as possible. If only a small portion of a negative or slide is enlarged the grain becomes more noticeable, no matter how fine-grained the film may be.

Contrast. The relationship between black or dark areas and white or light areas, referred to as contrast, also varies between films. In general,

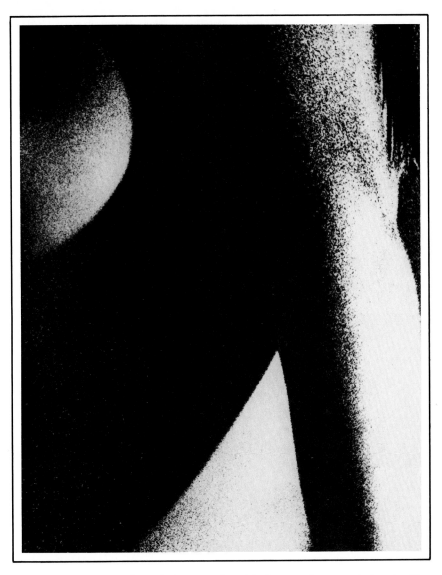

To enhance the graphic effect of this image, the original was made on very fast, grainy film. A contrasty print was made, then copied on a high contrast film. The resulting negative was then printed again on a high contrast paper. Photo: G. Kotler

slow films have more contrast than fast films. There is a greater degree of difference between tones; whites or light areas seem lighter, dark areas look blacker. Contrast in black-and-white films is easily controlled during the printing process, but in color the control of contrast is more difficult. Contrast increases as film is copied. Prints made from slides are more contrasty than the original slides. For the most pleasing results strive for normal contrast. However, if you want more contrast consider using films noted for their high inherent contrast, such as Kodak Technical Pan or Panatomic-X films.

Daylight-balanced color film produces an orange-yellow cast when exposed under tungsten light. A tungsten-balanced film would have produced more "normal" color, but that is not always the way to get the most expressive image. Photo: F. Leinwand.

Color Values

With color photography your personal taste in color values is important, because there are differences among various color films. This variation is especially noticeable with slide films.

Color Balance of Light and Film. Various sources produce light of different color qualities because they emit different combinations of visible wavelengths. The "color balance" of light can be expressed as a temperature on the Kelvin (K) scale; for example, a 500-watt photoflood lamp produces 3400 Kelvin light.

Color film emulsions are made with their sensitiviity matched to a particular kind of light. To get accurate color rendition you must use a properly matched film-light combination, or you must use a conversion filter on the camera lens to correct a mismatch.

Whenever possible, choose the color film for the type of light source you plan to use. If daylight and electronic flash will be used, the daylight color film, such as Kodacolor II or Kodachrome 25, will give the truest colors. When you will be using photoflood lamps select a film balanced for the 3400K color of photofloods, such as Kodachrome 40. When the light source will be quartz studio lamps (sometimes called tungsten-halogen), choose a film balanced for 3200K lights, such as Ektachrome 160 (tungsten).

Fast color slide film for tungsten light is available as Ektachrome 160, made for 3200K lights but also good with 3400K photofloods if you use a light amber No. 81A filter. Ektachrome 400, a daylight-type slide film, gives nice color quality even with unusual lighting.

Negative Films. All color negative films for 35mm cameras are balanced for daylight. If you must use color negative film with tungsten light sources (photofloods or quartz lamps), fit the camera with a bluish filter. There are two slightly different No. 80 filters, matched precisely to the type of light used. For photoflood lamps (3400K) use the No. 80B filter; for tungsten lights such as quartz/halogen (3200K) use the slightly darker No. 80A filter.

Fluorescent Light. When the lighting is from fluorescent lamps, color pictures are likely to have a greenish-yellow cast. To get rid of the tint from the fluorescents, use an FLD filter with daylight-type color film, or an FLB filter with tungsten type film. A few unusual types of fluorescent lamps have a color so close to daylight that they are acceptable for color photography.

Common reading lamps with tungsten bulbs give an orange tint to daylight film. Sometimes mixing tungsten lamps in the usual home fixtures with overhead fluorescents gives a lighting color that is very pleasing for documentary or informal photographs. The warm light from the tungsten bulbs gets rid of the greenish tinge of the fluorescents.

"Mismatching" Film and Light. The accompanying chart shows how to correct for mismatched film and light combinations.

For example, you can use tungsten-type film in daylight if you put an orange-toned No. 85 filter in front of the lens. Without the filter, tungsten color film used in daylight or with electronic flash gives blue-tinted results.

FILTERS TO MATCH COLOR FILM AND LIGHT SOURCE			
Light	**Color Film**		
	Daylight	*Tungsten, Type A* (3400K)	*Tungsten, Type B* (3200K)
Daylight; Electronic flash; Blue flashbulbs.	No filter	#85 filter	#85B filter
Tungsten 3200K	#80A filter	#82A filter	No filter
Tungsten 3400K	#80B filter	No filter	#81A filter

Using Different Films for the Same Subject

Photographers who frequently want to photograph the same subject on two or more types of film find it worthwhile to keep an extra camera body loaded with the second film. Changing between films with a cartridge-loading camera is easy. Advance the film one frame to protect the exposure you have just made and simply remove the cartridge from the camera. Whenever you want to use that film again, load the cartridge into the camera and advance the film one frame. Only one exposure will be wasted this way, without losing any of your other pictures.

Whenever you load or unload a camera, do it in subdued light. If you are outdoors, work in the shade or at least turn your back to the sun to shadow the camera. Be sure to keep partially exposed film in a lighttight container or wrapped in black plastic or aluminum foil until you use it again.

Kodachrome film, used for the picture at left, typifies the rendition of a normal color film for daylight use. Kodak Photomicrography color film, a specialized film with increased contrast, gives a very different look to the same scene. Photos: M. Fairchild.

Technique Tip: Changing Film in Mid-Roll

You can change from one film to another even before you finish the roll. Here are the steps to follow with most 35mm cameras:

1. Note the number of exposures taken already (film-counter position).
2. Press in rewind button.
3. *Slowly* rewind the film until you *feel* and *hear* the film pull free from the take-up spool. *Stop* rewinding as soon as you know the film has left the rewind; do not rewind further, or the film leader may wind all the way into the magazine.
4. Open the camera.
5. Remove the magazine. Wrap the leader around the magazine and secure it with a piece of tape so it cannot be pulled inside.
6. Write on the tape or leader how many exposures have been taken. Also note the ISO/ASA used if it is different from the normal rating.
7. Put the film into a plastic or metal film can with a tight top. Label the container.
8. Now your camera is free. Load the new type of film you wish to use.
9. Set the camera meter for the new ISO/ASA.
10. Proceed to take photographs.

When the time comes to reload the first roll of film, you must get it back to the same position it had when you decided to rewind. To do this, load the film as usual, then:

1. Put on the lens cap.
2. Set shutter to maximum speed.
3. Set *f*-stop to smallest possible opening.
4. Push the shutter release and advance the film repeatedly until you have gone one more frame than you had exposed before. For example, if the roll has 14 exposures on it from the previous time in your camera, advance it through 15 exposures with the lens cap on. The extra frame is to prevent an unwanted double exposure caused by any discrepancy in the total film travel between the two times you have loaded the film.
5. Set the ISO/ASA on the camera and finish the roll.

5

Exposure

Getting perfect exposures is easy with modern cameras and precision meters. You must remember to adjust the ISO/ASA setting correctly for the speed of the film just loaded. An advanced 35mm single-lens reflex camera is a versatile tool, but it must be programmed for the film you choose before the metering system can be expected to deliver the best average exposures. Simple cameras with cartridge-load films are adjusted automatically by the cartridge when it is put into the camera, but 35mm film magazines have no camera programming functions. You must manually set the film speed on the camera meter or accessory hand-held meter. Knowing the correct ISO/ASA rating is easy because most manufacturers mark it both on the package and the magazine of film itself.

Standard processing will produce pleasing results with the great majority of adequately lighted subjects when the film is exposed at the manufacturer's recommended ISO/ASA speed. That is, the speed and the processing assume a normal or average subject and exposure. In both slides and in prints from negatives, you can obtain a full range of tones, from very light to dark. However, correct exposure is rather critical with slide films. Negative films have more room for over- or underexposure before the pictures suffer.

For example, a negative color film can be overexposed or underexposed by two *f*-stops and still yield prints of acceptable quality. (The best quality usually results when the film is exposed precisely, according to the meter reading.) The degree to which a film can be over- or underexposed but still give acceptable pictures is called latitude. Negative films have more latitude than slide films; your exposure precision must be greater with slide films if you expect maximum quality.

"Correct" exposure of color film is a matter of the visual appeal of the final image. Some scenes are enhanced by the increased color saturation you can get by giving slightly less than the meter-indicated exposure. Photo: L. Brauner.

Camera Controls

Two mechanical parts of your camera control the exposure. One is the size of the lens opening, the aperture or *f*-stop. How the aperture is adjusted, what *f*-stop you use, determines how much light comes into the camera. The second camera control over exposure is the shutter speed.

The *f*-stop and shutter speed work together with mathematical precision. In most cases, if you choose fast shutter speeds you will need relatively large lens openings.

When the light falls upon the film for a very short time, as with fast shutter speeds, the light must be bright, more intense; hence the need for a large *f*-stop to let in more light. The opposite occurs with slow shutter speeds. When the light will hit the film for a relatively long time it can be less bright but still produce the correct exposure. A small *f*-stop reduces the brightness.

Exposure can be determined precisely by a light meter. The meter senses the amount of light, relates it to the film speed, and indicates a series of speeds and *f*-stop combinations, all of which will produce the same average exposure. For example, *f*/11 at 1/15 sec., *f*/5.6 at 1/60 sec., and *f*/2 at 1/500 sec. will all produce the same exposure. You can see the equivalent exposure combinations on most meter dials, or you can easily count them out on the chart given here.

Controlling Exposure by *f*-stop. Suppose the meter reading is *f*/5.6 at 1/60 sec., but you wish to use *f*/11. Find *f*/5.6 and count the number of steps to *f*/11: two. Next, find the shutter speed indicated by the meter, 1/60

Scenic subjects often call for sharpness in depth. You'll need to use a small f-stop to get as much sharpness as possible. Photo: J. Scheiber.

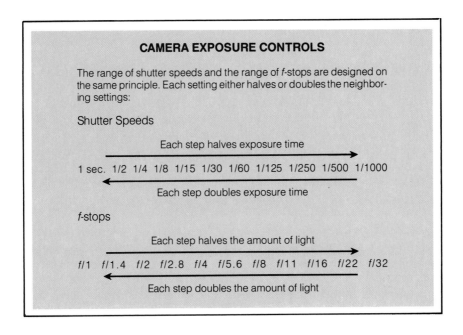

CAMERA EXPOSURE CONTROLS

The range of shutter speeds and the range of *f*-stops are designed on the same principle. Each setting either halves or doubles the neighboring settings:

Shutter Speeds

Each step halves exposure time →

1 sec. 1/2 1/4 1/8 1/15 1/30 1/60 1/125 1/250 1/500 1/1000

← Each step doubles exposure time

f-stops

Each step halves the amount of light →

f/1 *f*/1.4 *f*/2 *f*/2.8 *f*/4 *f*/5.6 *f*/8 *f*/11 *f*/16 *f*/22 *f*/32

← Each step doubles the amount of light

sec., and count the same number of steps, *but in the opposite direction.* Two steps takes you to 1/15 sec. So, *f*/11 at 1/15 sec. gives the same exposure as *f*/5.6 at 1/60 sec. Try it on the chart above.

Controlling Exposure by Shutter Speed. You can also choose a shutter speed rather than an *f*-stop. Again, the meter reading is *f*/5.6 at 1/60 sec., but now you want to use 1/500 sec. Count from 1/60 to 1/500: three steps. So count three steps in the opposite direction from *f*/5.6 to *f*/2. An exposure of *f*/2 at 1/500 sec. is the same as an exposure of *f*/5.6 at 1/60 sec.

Automatic Exposure Control. Cameras with automatic exposure control features contain built-in meters that let you choose one exposure factor while the camera automatically chooses the other factor, based on the meter's response to the subject brightness. An *aperture-preferred* (or aperture-priority) camera lets you choose the *f*-stop while it automatically selects the matching shutter speed. A *shutter-preferred* (priority) camera lets you choose the speed while it takes care of setting the lens aperture.

Depth-of-Field Control. If you want maximum sharpness near and far—called depth of field—use the smallest possible *f*-stop. But keep in mind the slow shutter speed that will require. An exposure of *f*/22 at 1/30 sec., say, will give overall sharpness only if the subject and camera are absolutely still. Otherwise, movement will cause a blurred image.

When you want the depth of field to be shallow, perhaps to put a distracting background well out of focus so it becomes a pleasing blur of color, use a wide aperture with an appropriately fast shutter speed.

Using Your Camera Meter

The built-in meters in modern single-lens reflex cameras read the light from behind the lens and the meter reacts to the light *reflected from* the subject; this is called reflected-light metering. Hand-held meters can read either the light reflected from the subject or all the light *falling on* the subject; the second is called incident-light metering. Some devices are sold that clip on the front of a lens to convert the camera's meter into an incident-light meter. When taking an incident-light reading, the meter is held at the *subject* position, pointed back toward where the camera will be. This technique ignores the actual subject brightness. Instead, an incident-light meter collects all the light falling on the subject, and uses that to provide an average exposure recommendation.

In contrast, a reflected-light reading—the type you will usually take with your built-in camera meter—is directly influenced by the subject brightness because the meter is pointed at the subject. The basic techniques for making and using reflected light meter readings are given in the box. In general, reflected-light readings give excellent results with negative as well as slide films, both black-and-white and color. Incident-light readings are most useful for determining color slide film exposures.

Technique Tip: Reflected-Light Metering Techniques

1. Set the meter to the ISO/ASA speed of the film.
2. Point the meter (or camera lens, for a built-in meter) at the subject from the camera direction. Outdoors, tilt down so that the sky occupies less than one-third of the area being read.
3. For *broad area subjects,* such as landscapes, and subjects with many areas of different brightness or color: expose both *black-and-white and color films* just as the overall meter reading indicates. This technique is best for the majority of fully lighted subjects.
4. For *single large area subjects,* with a small amount of background: expose *color films* as indicated by a meter reading taken from the most important color area; for *black-and-white films,* take a reading from the darkest important area (an area that is to be very dark, but not completely black), and give two stops *less* exposure than the meter indicates.
5. For *portraits:* Take a reading from the face. Expose *color films* as indicated by the meter. Expose *black-and-white films* one stop *more* than the meter indicates.

Except on overcast days, open sky is bright enough to throw off exposure readings. Tilt your camera or meter to eliminate the sky when making reflected-light readings for outdoor pictures. Photo: M. Fairchild.

A Meter Trick. There is an easy way to get an average reflected-light meter reading for a white or black subject, or a subject against a great expanse that is much brighter or darker than what you want to feature, or a subject that is too small to fill the meter reading area. The trick is to take the reading from a substitute subject.

The best substitute subject is a standard gray card (the Kodak Neutral Test Card, available in photo stores). If you do not have a gray card, you can use the palm of your hand instead. Proceed as follows.

1. Place the gray card at the subject position, or in the same kind of light that is falling on the subject.
2. Compose your picture of the subject and focus sharply. Then approach the gray card, without refocusing, until it fills most of the camera viewfinder (or hand-meter reading area). Your camera meter may be more sensitive in one particular area of the picture, such as in a center-weighted system. In that case the favored area, often a circle, fill with the card.
3. Adjust the camera exposure controls according to the meter reading from the gray card. If your camera is working on automatic, be sure to lock in the gray card meter reading so it will not change when you move back to your original position.
4. Remove the gray card, frame your photograph again, and make the exposure.
5. If you take the meter reading from the palm of your hand, held in the same light as the subject, give *one stop more* exposure than the meter indicates. (You can do this by using the next slower shutter speed, *or* the next larger *f*-stop, *or* by setting the meter to half the usual ISO/ASA film speed. Do only one of these things; see the next section.)

65

Good exposure is not a mystical subject. It is simply a matter of determining what average exposure should be, and then thinking about what is important in the picture. That will tell you how to adjust the exposure.

When your composition includes a wide range of brightnesses, adjust exposure to favor the most important part of the photograph. For example, a person with dark skin against a bright white sand beach or sparkling water will need more exposure than the surroundings if you want full detail in the face. That means the beach and water will be slightly overexposed when you provide the ideal exposure for your human subject. On the other hand, if the beach and water are most important, give the ideal exposure for the surroundings. You must decide what kind of picture you want. If you must have both the bright surroundings and the dark-skinned human subject perfectly exposed, you must add light to the human subject. Do this by using a reflector or a small electronic flash unit.

Of course, you must know how to adjust exposure accurately. Study your camera instruction book carefully. Some cameras have meter positions that program variations. For example, if you know that a general meter reading or automatic camera exposure will give one stop too little light, adjust the built-in meter to give a one-stop increase. This feature is usually written on the meter dial as + 1. To get one stop less exposure than the average meter reading, use the − 1 position. Thus, if you are photographing subjects against a dark background and your meter will be influenced by the expanse of darkness, set the meter to provide one stop less exposure. With such an adjustment the subjects will have greater detail, better color saturation, and the dark background will look dark, not gray.

Overriding the Fully Automatic Camera. If your camera is fully automatic, without any way to override the meter or hold in (lock) a meter reading taken from a gray card or close-up from the subject, then proceed as follows:

1. Decide how much more or less you want to expose the film. For example, one stop *more* exposure for peope in sunlighted snow.
2. Set the meter ISO/ASA dial to a speed setting one-half lower than the actual loaded film calls for. If you are using Kodacolor II with a usual rating of 100, but decide that the meter will give an exposure one stop too little—too dark—then set the meter dial for ISO/ASA 50. This adjustment will make the camera do what you want.
3. To get *less* exposure, set the meter for a *higher* film speed. Double the ISO/ASA number to get one stop less exposure. For two-stop changes multiply the original film speed by four for less exposure, or divide it by four for more exposure.
4. Remember to reset the meter for the usual rating when you are ready to photograph subjects of average reflectance or usual conditions again.

In some cases, simply setting the right exposure will not guarantee a good photograph. If your subject has important dark details, you may need to bring them out by using a small electronic flash unit or white reflector to throw some additional light into the shaded areas. Electronic flash fill was used in this picture—without it, the boy's hat would have cast a shadow on his face, rendering it too dark. Photo: A. Rakoczy.

Slight changes in exposure can cause marked differences in color rendition, especially with transparency film. The beach scene above was given normal exposure. This produced good color saturation and clearly defined detail in the highlights. To guarantee yourself proper exposure and good color saturation, "bracket" your exposures a half-stop in either direction. Photos: J. DiChello, Jr.

Bracketing Exposures

Professional photographers are in the habit of taking a photograph at the suggested meter reading plus additional frames with less exposure and more exposure. This is called bracketing. You should do the same, when the situation is unusual or when you are photographing something that cannot be captured again. Sometimes one of the frames that you took lighter or darker will be more pleasing than the meter-suggested average exposure. With negative film, bracket by a full *f*-stop or shutter speed; with slide film bracket by one-half stop or shutter speed.

For example, if you are using Kodacolor II print film and the meter suggests 1/60 sec. at *f*/11, take the suggested exposure. Then take another at 1/60 at *f*/8 (one stop more) and a third at 1/60 at *f*/16 (one stop less). If you are using a slide film such as Kodachrome 64 and the meter says 1/60 sec. at *f*/8, take the suggested exposure. Then take a second at 1/60 at *f*/6, and a third at 1/60 at *f*/10. You will not find these half-stop positions listed on the lens, but they occur halfway between the marked *f*-stops on either side of *f*/8. Some lens controls click into place at the halfway positions. For very important subjects on slide film bracket two half-stop steps in each direction: for example, at *f*/8, *f*/6, *f*/5.6, *f*/9, and *f*/11.

When transparencies are overexposed by a full stop, the colors become weak and washed-out. Detail disappears from the lightest areas of the scene.

One full stop of underexposure made the colors of this scene dull and muddy, with no clean whites and less detail in the dark areas.

Meter Readings and Light Directions

Your meter readings will vary depending upon the direction of the light. For example, the face of a person facing away from the light source will require more exposure than if the person were facing toward the source, assuming that the same amount of detail is desired in both cases. Certain adjustments must thus be made to ensure proper exposure.

Frontlight. For front-illuminated subjects of average reflectance simply use the meter-indicated exposure using the normal film rating. If the subject is very dark or very light adjust the suggested exposure by one-half to one stop or use a gray card to obtain the average exposure.

Backlight. Take a meter reading off the subject from close up, so the camera is not influenced by the backlight, or open the lens one to two *f*-stops more than the meter suggests for a subject in the same location but frontlighted. For example, you are outdoors on a bright day and a frontlighted subject needs 1/125 sec. at *f*/11, but you want to take a photograph with the sun *behind* the subject (backlighting). Take the exposure at 1/125 sec. opened up one stop to *f*/8 for light subjects, or two stops to *f*/5.6 for dark subjects.

Sidelight. For sidelighting, expose for the most important part of the composition. With negative film favor the shadows when setting your exposure, with slide film favor the bright areas. If you do not care about having detail in the shadows, just set meter readings from the bright portions. If there is too much contrast between the light and dark areas, so that the dark areas lose more detail than you desire, then add light to the shadows with reflectors. Outdoors, using a large white card or a sheet of aluminum foil as a reflector is much easier than trying to fill shadows with electronic flash.

Mixed Interior and Exterior Light. You may want to compose a photograph that includes a window view *and* an interior subject. Usually the difference between outdoor and indoor light intensity is much too great for any film to capture. Unless you can cut down the outside brightness or add light to the much darker interior, you must decide which part of the total composition should get the ideal exposure.

Low-Light Situations. Besides the unaverage situations created by subjects of very high or very low reflectance, you may have to photograph under unusual conditions such as at night. For powerful nighttime exposures with dark backgrounds but well-exposed lights, buildings, and windows, or for people on a stage lighted with spotlights, etc. try to get reflected-light meter readings taken when the subject almost fills the frame. If you can't get close, you could change to a telephoto lens to take a reading, then change back to the other lens to actually take the picture. If this is impossible consult the folder that comes packed with high-speed film.

Sunrises and Sunsets. For the best color saturation, take meter readings from the colored sky. (If you plan on photographing the sun before it is low on the horizon, or after it has risen, do not look through your finder directly at the sun. Focus the lens at infinity and simply point the camera toward the sun.) Meter readings taken off the just-rising sun or a fully colored setting sun close to the horizon will give excellent color, with some detail in the other parts of the picture and full detail in the sky.

If you want more detail in the land portion of your photograph, meter with the sun only partially in the frame, or open up one or two stops beyond suggested exposures taken from the sun. As with all unusual exposure situations you should bracket exposures.

To create this silhouette, the photographer based his exposure on a reflected meter reading of the water, ignoring the settings required for the "proper" exposure of the island. Photo: J. Howard.

6

Useful Accessories

Your camera and lens are the most important tools in creative photography, but some accessories will help you protect your equipment and get more creative results.

Straps

The first step to keeping your equipment in good condition is to use a sturdy strap that lets you carry the camera with minimum chance for dropping it. Look over the straps available at local camera stores. There are two key points to consider:

1. Is the strap strong enough for your camera and lens combination? Is the strap attachment (ring or clip) sturdy, secure?
2. Is the strap comfortable for you? Some ultra-wide straps are attractive and comfortable if you wear only one camera at a time but may be too wide or too hot if you plan on wearing two cameras. Many serious photographers carry one camera body holding color film and a second loaded with black-and-white. In such a case, one wide strap next to the neck, and a thinner, lightweight strap for the second camera might be more comfortable.

A carrying strap is a very important accessory, especially when you are involved in activities such as sailing, which can endanger your equipment. Without a strap around your neck, a sudden lurch of the boat could mean a damaged or lost camera. Make sure the strap you choose is both strong and comfortable enough to carry your camera for hours at a time. Photo: P. Bereswill.

Cases

A strap will let you carry your camera safely while shooting, but a case is necessary to protect it and other equipment between times. If you have only one camera with lens, and no assortment of accessories, then a tightly fitted everready case for your camera and lens is a good investment. An everready case is designed to fit a specific camera and lens combination with a minimum of bulk. A typical everready case comes in two parts: the base which screws into the camera tripod socket and may have an attached carrying strap, and a front cover that clips onto the base, then folds around in front to protect the whole lens and camera. To use the camera you unsnap the front, let it hang down out of the way or remove it, then proceed to take pictures.

Photographers with several lenses and perhaps with more than one camera usually attach the neck straps directly to the camera bodies, then protect the cameras and lenses in a separate shoulder bag or accessory case. The accessory case can be small, just large enough for the camera, a few filters, cleaning supplies, and an extra lens or two. Modern shoulder bags come in many styles, a number of which are well designed to protect your equipment. Some features are discussed below.

Hard or Soft? Soft, flexible cases, made of leather, plastic materials, canvas, or nylon are offered in many sizes. Some small flexible cases fit on a belt around your waist, some can be carried like a backpack, but most are designed as shoulder bags. The soft design means you can stuff many sorts of odd-sized equipment into the bag. Well-designed bags offer sturdy straps that continue around and under the bag, to fully support the weight.

Medium to high priced shoulder bags offer sturdy construction, outside pockets, and often have inner padding if the design is flexible. For additional protection of delicate lenses and filters, wrap fragile items in bubble plastic or keep them inside individual cases. Lenses can be carried loose in a shoulder bag without damage if each lens has a front and rear cap and is kept in an individual pouch or lens case. Filters usually come in plastic cases. Keep filters in their original cases, even though you may be putting them inside a compartment bag. Clean, scratch-free filters are important for sharp pictures.

Hard-sided bags, made from aluminum, leather over plastic or wood frame, plastic, and fiberglass, have the advantage of providing maximum protection for your equipment. Some have a fixed interior design to accommodate specific camera equipment. For example, a few have metal plates in the bottom to which you can attach your lenses, using the same bayonet arrangement as used on the camera body. Other hard cases offer foam inserts which you cut out to fit the equipment you usually carry.

One handy hard case, available in tough fiberboard or aluminum construction, has moveable compartments padded with foam. You can change the size of the individual spaces within the case, according to the equipment you wish to carry. Some hard cases are made to be set down flat, then

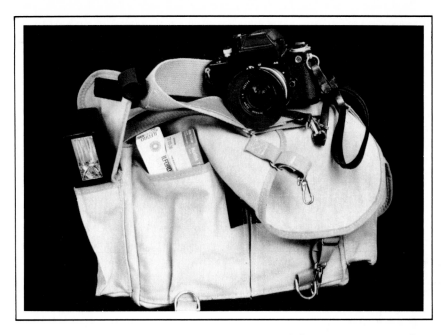

Camera bags and cases are made in a variety of materials. Soft bags are more convenient to use and lighter to carry; hard cases provide better protection for your delicate photographic equipment. Photo: C. M. Fitch

opened like a suitcase. Others are designed as shoulder bags, with a zipper, Velcro, latch, or snap-closing tops. These are best for field work where you must move around yet be able to get at your equipment fast.

Leather, Cloth, Plastic, Metal? Choose an accessory camera bag made from a material that will endure under the anticipated conditions. If you plan to carry several lenses and a body or two under very humid conditions, a metal or plastic case with watertight closure gaskets is a wise investment. Frequent travelers also appreciate hard cases that protect delicate equipment when the case is pushed under airline seats or knocked around in the usual activity of moving from one place to the next.

Nature photographers and backpackers who want a case with minimum weight and maximum flexibility will do well with a cloth shoulder bag, perhaps of tough nylon. If most of your work is indoors, a flat case is usually practical. With a top-opening case that has either foam cut-outs or padded partitions you can see and reach everything quickly.

Leather is lovely to feel but not a practical case material if you live in a warm, humid climate. Aluminum may discolor and oxidize if frequently exposed to salt water. Under wet, warm conditions fiberglass materials are most resistant to deterioration although some of the metal clasps may tarnish or rust after a while.

Whatever the material examine construction and workmanship carefully. A well-constructed case that fits your working style is excellent insurance.

Filters

Certain filters are extremely useful for general photography.

You can take meter readings directly through most filters for color photography, so no special exposure considerations are required. Meter readings through black-and-white filters are not likely to be accurate; instead you must compensate exposure by the amount indicated by the *filter factor*. This is a multiplier usually marked on the filter rim, or indicated in the film instruction sheet. Either multiply the shutter speed by the factor, or open the lens aperture an equivalent number of *f*-stops, as follows:

Factor	Open lens aperture
2X	1 stop
3X	1½ stops
4X	2 stops
6X	2½ stops
8X	3 stops

Skylight Filters. For color photography, most knowledgeable photographers use an ultraviolet absorbing skylight (No. 1A) filter. This serves two purposes. First, it protects the lens elements from physical damage. Even frequent cleaning will cut down on a lens' sharpness. When a skylight filter is damaged or worn, you have only an inexpensive filter to replace, not a costly lens. Second, the slight pink color of the skylight filter greatly improves color photographs taken outdooors under blue skies. Color film records more blue from the sky than our eyes see, partly because films are sensitive to ultraviolet. The skylight filter absorbs the excess blue

Photographing where there is much reflected light often leads to a lack of saturation in the colors. Photo: R. Mickelson.

and UV; however, its effect is so slight that no exposure compensation is required.

Polarizers. Besides the skylight filter you will find a polarizer very helpful. The polarizer can be used with color film to reduce reflected light, thus greatly improving color fidelity. Without a polarizer, outdoor photographs are likely to show white-tinged reflected light rather than true colors, especially in the sky, water, and from foliage. The polarizer eliminates much of this reflected light, thus letting the film record actual colors. Skies become rich blue, foliage a saturated green, bark a rich brown. Since the polarizer takes away some light, you must compensate by exposing one to two *f*-stops more. Most modern SLR cameras have metering systems that automatically compensate for what you attach in front of the lens. However, a few metering systems do not provide correct automatic readings through a polarizer. Your camera instruction book will point this out, should it be the case.

A polarizer reduces reflected light to let the film record colors full strength. You must increase exposure one to two stops when using a polarizer to compensate for the light it blocks. Photo: R. Mickelson.

Color Conversion. After the skylight and polarizer filters you should choose filters that are required for your specific work. For example, if you wish to use tungsten-type color film but frequently want to finish or start a roll under daylight conditions you will need a color conversion filter.

Without these conversion filters to match the light to the color balance of the film, you will get off-color results. Tungsten-type film used in daylight yields bluish results. Daylight-balanced color film exposed under tungsten illumination gives orangey results. If you want to settle on just one film, choose a tungsten-type and use a conversion filter outdoors. The greater intensity of daylight will make it easier to compensate the exposure for the filter without having to use excessively large *f*-stops or slow shutter speeds.

Filters for Fluorescent Lights. Color film, either daylight or tungsten type, exposed under fluorescent lamps, comes out with an unattractive yellowish-green tinge. If you must take color photos under fluorescent illumination use an FL filter to get more pleasing tones. The FL-D filter is made for daylight-balanced film, and the FL-B is made for tungsten- (bulb) balanced film. Both filters require one stop more exposure.

Filters for Black-and-White Photography. Black-and-white photography requires more strongly colored filters than color photography. Blue, red, yellow, green and orange filters are useful. For dramatic dark skies combine a red filter with a polarizer. A general rule in black-and-white photography is that filters render their own color *lighter* (in the gray scale) than other colors.

The photos below are black-and-white renditions of the color photo at left. The photo below left was taken with no filter. The photo below right was taken with a red filter, which lightened the reds, yellows, oranges and magentas, while darkening the blues and greens.

Skies in black-and-white scenes can be dramatically darkened by combining a red filter with a polarizing filter. Photo: H. Weber.

Tripods

Keeping your camera and lens steady is the main function of a tripod. At shutter speeds below 1/60 sec. most photographers have difficulty getting maximum sharpness because the camera moves slightly during the hand-held exposure. Using a tripod is the best way to reduce camera and lens shake. Indoors the tripod will usually eliminate all camera movement, unless the floor is vibrating from construction, traffic, loud music, or sounds.

Outdoors the tripod is also useful in reducing camera shake, although in heavy winds some camera and lens movement may still be present. If you plan to use slow shutter speeds outdoors get the most rugged, practical tripod. Very lightweight tripods are easy to carry but under windy conditions, or with a long telephoto lens, they are much too shaky.

Tripods are also good for precise composition. Even when you can take exposures at medium to fast shutter speeds, or with electronic flash, you will find a tripod an advantage in getting just what you want in each frame.

Even with your camera on a sturdy tripod you may make the camera shake slightly by pushing the shutter release too vigorously. To avoid this, use a cable release to set off the shutter.

Tripod Features. Tripods come in numerous designs. The type best for you depends on how and where the tripod will be used. For outdoor use, you should have a tripod that will not jam if soil or other dirt gets in the legs. Indoors, a tripod that has rubber feet or casters may be useful.

How the camera fastens on the tripod head also varies. Most common are tripods with a single screw that engages the tripod socket on the bottom of your camera. Another attachment system uses a plate that fastens first to the camera tripod socket, then drops into place on the tripod head.

This is especially so with tabletop photography, where the precise placement of objects is so important, and in copy work. In portrait photography a tripod is useful for getting a series of similar photos, including the exposure bracketing commonly done by serious photographers.

This system is useful if you frequently change from one camera body to another. The accessory plate attachment is also handy if you must work fast, under cold conditions, with gloves, or with a long, heavy lens. Most mounting plates can be very tightly fastened to the camera base, thus giving better traction than the single direct screw-in method. Some tripod heads tend to let a camera tilt down when fitted with a long telephoto lens and turned to a vertical position. Tripods with accessory mounting plates provide better support for cameras in the vertical position.

Other tripod options that may be useful in your work include a built-in bubble level to help retain straight horizons and a multiple-position head that swings (pans) from side to side, tilts left, right, up and down, and permits easy changes between vertical and horizontal camera positions.

If you are interested in the sharpest possible photographs, a tripod is indispensable. A cable release will further reduce the risk of camera shake.

Avoid tripods that have knobs or screws without locking washers, especially if you will travel with the tripod. Vibrations from a car or plane can cause unsecured knobs to drop loose. A cable release screws into the shutter button; it sets off the shutter when you push on the cable plunger. By the time this force reaches the camera it is weak enough to avoid making the camera shake. For slow shutter speeds a cable release is an especially useful accessory to your tripod-mounted camera. On rare occasions when a cable release is not at hand use the camera's self-timer to set off the shutter. This is a practical way to let handling vibrations subside before the shutter makes the actual exposure; of course the camera must be on a tripod or other firm support.

If you want to take low-angle views, or to get close to the ground (as in nature photography) pick a tripod that spreads to a very low position or has a reversing center column. Some tripods are designed to permit this close-to-the-ground work easily. If you like high-angle effects choose a model that permits tall extensions without becoming unsteady.

An adjustable center post is convenient for precise composition. Set the three legs to a basic height, then raise the center post for final composition. With any tripod use the largest leg extensions before pulling out the thinner ones. This will provide maximum sturdiness at any required height.

Flash Equipment

With flash equipment you will almost always have adequate illumination for the photographs you want to make. Not having to rely on available light, you will get more of the photographs you want.

Electronic Flash. A small, portable electronic flash unit is certainly useful. Modern electronic flash units accept AC power through adapters, or use disposable batteries or rechargeable cells. Many models offer automatic operation, some with several possible *f*-stops in automatic mode. Units of moderate power are so small that you can carry them in a shoulder bag or big pocket.

Electronic flash is useful for stopping fast-moving action. When your camera is used with electronic flash the exposure is usually controlled by the intensity of the flash burst. The effective exposure speed may range from 1/750 sec. up to 1/50,000 sec. or more on some automatic units. Naturally this ultra-fast burst of light "freezes" the subject motion.

Flash Recycling. Read the instruction book that comes with your flash unit. Most modern units have circuitry that conserves power when it is not required (thyristor circuitry). This type of design is the most efficient, extends battery life, and permits you to work faster. An electronic flash needs time to recycle, or build up power, between flashes. On auto mode

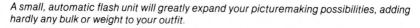

A small, automatic flash unit will greatly expand your picturemaking possibilities, adding hardly any bulk or weight to your outfit.

this time may be only a fraction of a second but on manual the required recycling time between flashes may be six or more seconds. The recycle time for manual use, in which the full power possible is released at each flash, is longer because the maximum power must be rebuilt after each exposure. As batteries get weaker the recycle time increases. If you plan to take flash pictures in rapid succession, perhaps with a motor drive, choose an electronic flash unit that offers fast recycling time at the output power you want. All units that accept AC recycle faster on that power than on batteries.

Other Flash Accessories. Portable electronic flash units can be fitted with several useful accessories. To diffuse the light you can add frosted translucent plastic or a blow-up frosted balloon-like device in front of the flash. Some flash units accept a small white card from which you can bounce the flash because the active flash head is designed to tilt up. Colored plastic or gelatin filters in front of the flash are fun for special effects, or even to match the flash to tungsten-type color film. A conversion filter can be used on the camera lens if the flash is your only light source. A salmon-colored gel, made to match a No. 85 filter color, will let you use the electronic flash in combination with other light sources that do not require filtration for tungsten-type film.

Select an electronic flash unit that gives adequate power for the films you want to use. If your favorite film is Kodachrome 25 and you want maximum depth of field you will need an electronic flash unit with enough power to provide small *f*-stops, but as the light-to-subject distance increases the flash must be much more powerful.

Other Considerations for Electronic Flash. Besides the basic power of an electronic flash unit, these other features should be considered when selecting the unit best suited to your applications: Does the electronic flash fit your camera easily? You may want to use the flash in a hot shoe connection. Can the flash be removed from the camera? Is the connecting cord (sync cord) long enough? Is it replaceable? Does the flash head turn, tilt, or rotate? You may want to bounce the light off an umbrella or white ceiling. Can the flash head be fitted with accessory diffusers to soften the light? How many batteries does the flash need? Will the unit also work off household electric current? Does it accept the current found in some other countries you may visit? Is the flash powerful enough for your use? Too powerful? If the unit is automatic, how many *f*-stop choices does it offer in each distance range? What are they for the ISO/ASA you want?

Consider an electronic flash made especially for your specific camera brand or model. Some of these dedicated flash units offer added convenience of finder ready-light, off-the-film metering, automatic shutter speed adjustment.

With any electronic flash attachment, read the instructions carefully, then take a test roll with notes on each exposure made. The exposure dial recommendations may not match your preference for ideal exposure, color saturation, shadow detail, etc.

7

Adding Light

What is the best way to add light to a subject? The answer depends on what light is already available, and what you want to accomplish with the light.

If you want to reduce contrast by filling in dark shadows formed by a constant light source such as the sun or a lamp, then a reflector is the best way to add light in the darker portion of your composition. The advantage of using reflectors is that you see what they are doing before you take the picture, in contrast to what happens when you fire a flash unit. Only larger, relatively expensive electronic flash units have model/focusing lights that let you preview where the light will fall. The popular portable electronic flash units make a burst that is so fast you cannot predict the final effect. This is why using a reflector for fill-light is often better than using a flash.

Strong sidelight, whether from the sun or electronic flash, can cause unpleasantly deep shadows on one side of the subject. These can be softened considerably by using a white reflector to "fill in" the shadow portions of the scene. Photo: P. Bereswill.

Reflector Materials. Suitability of reflector material depends upon several factors. In black-and-white photography any reflective material that bounces light where you want it is suitable. A ceiling or wall can be used as a bounce surface, but here we are considering *portable* reflectors that you can position freely. The best approach is to choose a reflector material that will serve both color and black-and-white work.

In color photography you must use a neutrally colored surface, such as white or silver. If you bounce light from a colored surface the resulting light will carry a color tint. For example, a light blue card used to bounce sunlight into the shadows will produce unattractive blue in the shadow areas. Silver surfaces are the most versatile for reflecting light. Reflector material offered for photographic use comes in flexible sheets with a tough plastic base. Various textures are available to change the quality of reflected light.

Umbrellas. Light bounced from a light-colored or white umbrella gives a soft wraparound effect with very open shadows. When the umbrella is placed to one side of the subject the light is directional enough to show texture and cause some shadows on the opposite side. As the um-

To flood his model with soft but intense light, the photographer shown here bounced the light from five electronic flash heads into white-surfaced umbrellas. The backs of the umbrella reflectors are black to ensure that all of the light reflects onto the subject.

A reflector is an easy way to get two light sources from one. Outdoors, use a white card or cloth to reflect sunlight onto the shaded portions of the subject. The larger and more matte-surfaced the reflector, the more diffuse the fill light will be. Photo: C.M. Fitch.

brella is moved toward the subject, providing reflected light from the front of the camera position, the shadows become weaker and the light flatter.

Umbrellas made for photographic applications come in different surfaces. As with other reflective surfaces the texture influences the light quality and brightness. Silver Mylar or silvery fabric gives bright light; white fabric gives a less sharp, light that is about one stop less bright. Frosted translucent umbrellas are used to diffuse direct (unbounced) light from flash, lamps, or the sun.

Bouncing a flash into an umbrella takes about one *f*-stop of light away from the flash brightness. For example, if the light from an electronic flash unit pointed directly at the subject requires an exposure at *f*/11, the exposure for the same flash bounced into a silver umbrella will be *f*/8.

Cloth Reflectors. Some photographic reflectors are made from fabrics coated with reflective material. The fabrics fit over lightweight metal frames which in turn can be fastened to stands. One of the advantages of these reflectors is that the fabrics can be folded to fit into small cases while the stands can be collapsed and fitted into heavy-duty plastic carrying cases. In addition, electronic flash units or lamps can be fastened to the stands, then pointed at the reflector for bounce lighting. You can vary the fabrics to change the quality of reflected light. A super silver surface gives sharp light and distinct shadows, while a plain silver surface provides a softer light that is ideal for portraits; a gold fabric warms the light, soft white gives very flat fill, and a translucent fabric lets you aim a light directly *through* it for a diffused effect. The translucent type is also useful to direct sun outdoors.

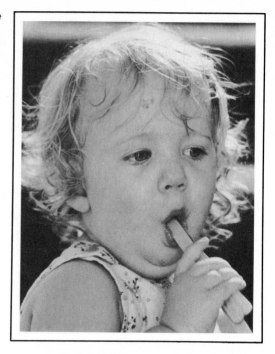

Strong sunlight directly over the subject causes harsh shadows under the eyes, nose, and chin. Use a portable electronic flash unit to add light to these areas. Photo: J. Peppler.

Sunlight plus Flash

Flash Fill. Even when the sun is bright you may want to add light in the shadow areas that occur when the sun strikes the subject at an angle. When a reflector is impractical to use or not available, you can use a portable electronic flash unit for this purpose. The technique of blending electronic flash with available sunlight is called flash fill. To do this proceed as follows:

1. Determine the *f*-stop required for correct exposure in the daylight, using the proper shutter speed required for electronic flash sync. This is usually between 1/60 and 1/125 sec. in 35 mm SLR cameras. As an example, assume that the flash sync speed is 1/60 sec. and that exposure in the sun at 1/60 is *f/*8. Set your camera for this exposure.
2. Now adjust your flash unit to give about one stop less light. Modern electronic flash units often have variable output settings, usually at one-fourth, one-half, and full power. This is a very helpful feature for efficient fill-in flash outdoors. The dial on such units shows which power setting to use for full exposure at various flash-to-subject distance and *f*-stop combinations. Using a *lower* power setting will reduce the flash exposure.
3. In this case let us assume you are 2 meters (6½ ft.) from the subject. The dial on the flash says that at full power with the film you are using, the flash exposure should be *f/*8, the same as for the available light. If you use this full power setting the flash will equal

the brightness of the sunlight, giving a flat, artificial look, without any shadows or modeling. To avoid this, adjust the power ratio to half, thus giving enough light to expose the film at f/5.6.

4. Compose and take the photograph, using the meter-suggested camera exposure of f/8 at 1/60 sec. (sunlight reading). Because the flash is used at f/5.6, a power *weaker* than the available sunlight exposure, it will fill in or lighten the dark shadows without washing them out or overpowering the natural light.

Flash as the Main Light Source. To expose pictures mainly by electronic flash, with little effect from the available light, be sure that the flash provides light at least two f-stops brighter than the available light exposure.

If you use flash on a moving subject when the available light is equal to that produced by the flash, you are likely to get a double image. The flash gives one exposure in a fraction of a second, then the available light causes another exposure on the same frame as the camera shutter is closing. This effect is called a ghost image or ghosting.

Since correct balancing of electronic flash with sunlight is often difficult, you may find that reflectors are an easier approach to adding light.

Technique Tip: Reducing the Brightness of Non-Variable Flash

If your flash unit does not have variable power, you can still reduce its light for fill-in flash. There are two simple ways to do this:

Cover the flash head with a layer of white cloth such as a pocket handkerchief. Each layer of cloth reduces the light about one stop in intensity.

OR

Move the flash unit farther from the subject. First, using the flash dial or instruction sheet, determine the correct flash-to-subject distance for normal (full) exposure. Multiply that by 1.4 to get the new distance for a one-stop reduction in flash exposure. If you are using negative film, you can simply move camera and flash together to the new distance, and specify the desired cropping and framing of the subject when you have an enlarged print made. If you are using slide film, you will have to keep the camera at the position that gives the desired composition and move only the flash unit. This means you will need a sync connecting cord long enough to reach the camera, and human or mechanical assistance for holding the flash unit in position.

Flash Outdoors at Night

The exposure dial on electronic flash units and the guide numbers given in instruction booklets are based on using the flash indoors. When you use flash outside at night there is no other light to add to the exposure and, more importantly, there are no ceilings or walls to reflect some of the flash onto the subject. You may well find that non-automatic flash exposures determined by the dial or guide number are one to two f-stops less than ideal when you work outdoors at night. The best way to learn how to deal with this situation is by practical test.

Take some test frames at a fixed distance between light and subject but at several different f-stops. Be sure to record the f-stop used for each frame. Then examine the processed results to determine a new "nighttime" guide number. Since guide numbers are correlated with flash-to-subject distance, you will find it easiest to do the test with the subject 3 meters (10 ft.) from the flash.

1. At night outdoors arrange a subject 3 meters from the flash. Usually the flash will be on the camera so you can read the distance directly from the lens focusing distance scale.
2. Find the recommended guide number for the film you are using. For this example we will say that the guide number with your unit is 80 for an ISO/ASA 64 film. That means an f/8 lens opening at 10

The illumination of small electronic units falls off drastically in non-reflective surroundings, such as those encountered outdoors at night. You can use this to create the kind of profile effect shown here by moving the flash unit off camera (in this case 90° to the left) and placing it at the far limits of its range. Photo: J. Peppler.

Taking flash pictures outdoors at night requires extra exposure, because you do not have light reflected from nearby surfaces, as you do indoors. To test for this, set up a subject at night 10 feet from your camera and flash. Make an exposure based on the regular guide number, then give one stop more, two stops more, and three stops more. The f-number of the best exposure, multiplied by 10, will give you the correct guide number for outdoor work. For example, if it was f/8, the guide number is 80. Photo: M. Fairchild.

feet (10 feet divided into the guide number of 80). The shutter is set at the electronic sync speed.

3. Take a series of photographs from 3 meters at f-stops of f/4.5, f/5.6, f/8, f/11. You do not need to test smaller f-stops because you will need more, not less, exposure at night outdoors.

4. Study the pictures when they are processed. Choose the frame that looks best to you in terms of color saturation and general exposure. Multiply the f-number used for that frame by the flash-to-subject distance to get your new nighttime guide number. If the f/8 exposure looks best to you then the recommended guide number (80) is suitable. However, if the f/5.6 exposure looks best (very likely in this night situation outdoors), then the effective guide number for your unit outside at night is 5.6 x 10 = 56.

Note that when electronic flash is used as the only source of light the fast burst will determine the actual speed at which the frame is exposed. This is why even small portable electronic flash units can stop fast action. Even if the subject moves during the exposure it will only be shown for a brief fraction of a second as the flash goes off. For example, one popular portable flash unit fires at 1/1000 sec. on manual and up to 1/50,000 sec. in some auto modes—more than enough to "freeze" moving subjects and eliminate any chance of camera shake showing.

Flash Indoors

Inside, flash can bounce off nearby surfaces, helping to fill in shadows and adding some light to the overall exposure. Rooms with low white ceilings and light-colored walls often give better results for indoor flash photos than rooms with high or dark ceilings. If the walls and ceilings are white you can use them as a surface for bounce flash.

Direct flash gives a crisp light with distinct dark shadows. Determine non-automatic direct flash exposures from the usual guide number or the unit dial or chart. If you prefer a softer light with more open shadows aim the flash at the wall opposite your subject, or at the ceiling several feet in front of the subject. When photographing people, be sure not to bounce the light off the ceiling directly above the subject because this causes dark shadows under the eyes.

By "bouncing" flash illumination off a light wall or ceiling, you can augment the light indoors without changing the natural look of the existing light. Photo: J. Peppler.

Direct flash is a fine way to photograph parties and other social events indoors. It helps to use a bracket or other adapter that will let you position the flash several inches up and over the lens. Photo: J. Scheiber.

For pleasing bounce flash illumination off a white wall, position the person .61–.91 meters (2–3 ft.) away from the wall, then aim your flash at the wall slightly higher than the person's head. Remember that with color film you should only bounce light from white or silver surfaces if you want natural color. Light bounced off colored surfaces comes back tinted with an identical hue.

Bouncing the flash reduces its intensity. For manual-mode exposures you will need from ½ to 1½ stops additional exposure, depending upon the room size and the total flash-to-subject distance, (that is, the combined distance from the flash to the bounce surface to the subject). Shooting a test-and-experiment roll of film is the best way to learn about controlling bounce flash. Automatic flash units will give proper exposures when the light sensor is *at the camera position* and is aimed *at the subject,* not at the bounce-light ceiling or wall.

Multiple Flash

When using multiple flash units only one need be attached to the sync socket or hot shoe of your camera. To fire the additional units equip each one with an automatic slave switch (also called a remote trigger). These small devices see the light when the main unit goes off and cause the remote flash units to fire simultaneously. An example of using several flash units for a portrait would include a main flash aimed at the person from near the camera, a second flash for fill light on the opposite side (either farther away or at lower power for about one stop less light than the main flash), and a third flash aimed at the subject from behind and above to illuminate the hair. Some photographers also like to aim a light at the background.

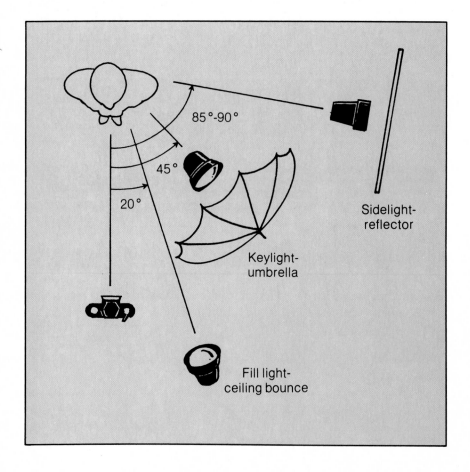

85°-90°

45°

20°

Sidelight-
reflector

Keylight-
umbrella

Fill light-
ceiling bounce

Two or even three lights are sometimes required to produce seemingly simple effects. In this instance, the photographer used three flash heads—one direct, and two bounced from reflective surfaces, as shown in the diagram on the opposite page. Photo: R. Von Kaenel.

8

Creating Successful Photographs

Owning good equipment and understanding its operation is only the beginning for a creative photographer. Photographs cease being snapshots when you begin to control the visual effectiveness of what appears in the frame. As a beginning you can vary the angle of each picture to best express your ideas about the subject. Include objects that add interest; give subjects a prop or something to do to make a visual statement; compose each photograph for maximum impact.

As a photographer you must sometimes capture fast action and get on film what cannot be controlled or easily repeated. At such times experience with composition, lens use, and technical control of your equipment are of primary importance. Catching fast movements or the right expressions is easy when you have mastered technique enough to be free to concentrate on your subject. This chapter covers some important points to consider for every picture. They apply to capturing fast-moving events and to creating photographs when you have more time as well.

To capture fast-breaking situations on the street you must be able to compose the picture and operate your camera quickly. Practicing the loading, unloading, focusing, setting exposure, changing lenses, etc. of your camera equipment will eliminate picture-losing fumbles and free you to concentrate on the contents of your photographs. Photo: C. Child.

Make use of the various elements in your images by moving around and seeing which placement looks best to you. Symmetry, balance, and near-far relationships are just some of the things you might watch for when composing. If you cannot get the arrangement you want by moving around, using another lens might improve your picture. Photo: B. Krist.

Composition

How you arrange the elements in your photographs—the final composition—determines the power of each image. Sloppy arrangement hides meaning, blurs your intent, and may even keep viewers from seeing your main subject.

Angle Around. Before taking a photograph look at the subject from various angles. Not only is one side usually more revealing or attractive, but you can make that best side look even better by choosing a complimentary angle. With people, a straight-on view is usually not as pleasant as a slightly turned pose.

Many buildings are more interesting when viewed from one corner, but some symmetrical buildings such as certain houses of worship, museums and other public buildings often look best seen straight on. Pictures of buildings may also be more interesting if you include people in the composition to indicate scale and foreground elements to add a sense of depth.

Composing with Lenses. Remember also that wide-angle lenses show a great deal around the subject; telephoto lenses have a narrower view, and that can be useful in background control.

Suppose that you want to photograph a person against a rather small section of hedge, an attractive fence, or a background of limited size. The view through your normal 50mm lens at the desired distance shows that the composition is good, but includes unwanted material off to both sides of your picture area. You could solve the problem by moving in closer, if that is possible, but that might make part of the subject larger than desired.

A better way around this problem is to narrow the field of view by using a longer lens from the original camera position. In this situation a 100 or 105mm lens would be ideal. The moderate telephoto focal length will provide the image size you want, but the narrower angle of view will take in only the desired amount of background.

 Technique Tip: Basics of Good Picture-Making

1. Are you close enough to the subject? Is it big enough to be seen clearly? To establish its own importance?
2. What do you see in the background? If you do not like what you see, shift the angle or blur the details by using a wider *f*-stop for less depth of field.
3. What angle have you picked? Children often look best when seen from their own height, some subjects are best shown from above, others from a lower angle.
4. Is the quality of light pleasing? If not then consider diffusing the light to soften it, or adding fill-light. Outdoors decide whether waiting for another time of day would improve the picture.
5. Does the direction and quality of the light help or hinder your photographic ideas?
6. Would a different lens make the photograph more powerful?
7. Are the colors pleasing? Are important elements likely to stand out as you wish? Or might they blend too much in the final picture?
8. How might you improve the composition?
9. Is your subject ready to be photographed, or should you spend some time preparing it before exposing film?
10. Are all your technical priorities taken care of? Even professionals may forget to load film, turn on a flash unit, or set the correct ISO/ASA speed on the meter.

Backgrounds

Careful selection and control of backgrounds will help make your photographs outstanding. A lovely flower seen in color against a misty haze of foliage is dramatic. The same flower pictured against perfectly sharp stems and a whole garden bed of competing blooms becomes a busy snapshot. Backgrounds can be controlled in two basic ways: either de-emphasize unwanted backgrounds by throwing them out of focus, or change the background behind the subject. Changing the background may be as simple as shifting the camera angle to put the subject in front of something more pleasing or appropriate. Well-chosen backgrounds should either be neutral, to put full attention on your main subject, or they should add to the overall power and meaning of your photograph. An example of a neutral background would be plain black or white cloth or paper used behind a flower or a brown panel behind a portrait subject. Neutral backgrounds are most useful when you are creating photographs under controlled conditions, as in your home or studio. However, while such backgrounds insure visibility and clear display by simplifying the setting, they remove the subject from its natural context. Natural or environmental backgrounds keep the subject in context.

Technique Tip: Depth of Field

A major expressive control in your pictures is sharpness — not just sharp focus on the main subject, but how sharp foreground and background details are as well. The near-to-far range of sharpness in the picture is called depth of field. You can choose great depth of field for sharp details throughout the picture, or shallow depth of field to concentrate attention on the subject and to de-emphasize other details by blurring them. You can achieve this kind of control as follows:

To increase depth of field
(1) Use a smaller lens aperture (higher *f*-number setting)
(2) Make the image smaller, either by moving farther away, or by changing to a shorter focal length lens

To decrease depth of field
(1) Use a larger lens aperture
(2) Make the image bigger, either by moving closer, or by changing to a longer focal length lens.

For the greatest amount of change, combine the two controls listed for each technique.

Narrow depth of field will help keep viewer concentration on the in-focus subject. When working close-up to your subject, depth of field is quite shallow, simplifying the technique for you. Photo: R. Sammon.

Environmental Backgrounds. Make natural backgrounds work for you when you take documentary photographs. On location, in homes, outdoors, in offices, during travels, you seldom have the freedom or time to arrange neutral backgrounds. These are the times that your talent with composition and depth-of-field control will help. With photographs of people consider including environmental details that make visual statements about the person.

Outdoors you have control over the background by using two basic controls. One is your angle of view. The angle you shoot from can place subjects against a background of your choice. The second is depth-of-field control. Remember that the smaller *f*-stops offer maximum sharpness behind the subject, while the more open *f*-stops limit depth of field, which puts the background out of focus.

Seamless Paper Backgrounds. Use a roll of seamless paper to form a neutral background behind and under your subjects. Narrow rolls 142cm wide by 11m long (52 in. × 36 ft.) are the most practical for home or small studio use. However, if you plan on photographing people full-length, or large subjects, you might need the wider 272cm (107 in.) rolls, also offered in 11m lengths. Papers are available in over 30 different colors, including a bright, pure white, deep black, and medium sky-blue.

If you enjoy doing portraits or tabletop photography of crafts, flowers, models, or still-life compositions, you will find constant use for seamless paper. Most of the product and catalog-model illustrations you see in publications are done on seamless paper. By varying the quantity of light on the paper you can change its color saturation.

Cardboard Backgrounds. When you need a controlled background only behind the subject, and not under it, you can use big sheets of colored mounting board, sold in art stores. A useful size is 81 × 101cm (30″ × 40″). This is large enough to provide a background for individual head-and-shoulder portraits.

Hold the stiff card with a swivel hook hanger that has two strong clips at each end. These are sold in some stores for hanging clothes and in art stores for hanging paintings until the paint dries. Another way to hang the cards behind your subject is with large spring clips sold in stationery stores. These usually have a hole on top through which you can fasten plastic-coated wire or strong string to tie the board on a background pole. When you want a high-angle view, looking directly down on a subject, place the card flat on the floor. Compose the subject toward the center of the card, then photograph from above.

Custom Backgrounds. You can customize your backgrounds by painting them with watercolors or by making blurs of different hues with pastel chalk. Arrange the paper or card far enough behind your subject so that it will be out of focus, to put full attention on your subject. Besides the custom-colored backgrounds you might experiment with silver or gold Mylar to get a water-like reflection of your subject on the background. This is attractive with flowers and sometimes with tabletop photography of crafts and antiques. Velvet and other fabrics may be useful in your work. Choose fabrics that look nice with the lighting you use.

To avoid distracting background shadows, pull down the paper from behind the subject, then roll it along the floor or over the table enough so that the subject can be placed on the paper at least 1 meter (3 ft.) in front of the vertical background section. If the subject is placed closer to the paper backing shadows are likely to fall within view on the background. Remember that carefully composed shadows *may* form an important part of a composition, but you should want them and should put them where they will add to the power of the photograph.

If your subject is simple enough, a wide variety of backgrounds may be suitable. The custom background adds some contrasting colors to the fairly monochromatic flowers. A solid-color background made with either a big piece of cardboard or paper would place more concentration on the flower. Background color should complement the color(s) of the subject. Photos: C.M. Fitch.

9

Practical Techniques for Planning Pictures

Creating powerful photographs begins with the selection of appropriate equipment. Experienced photographers assemble all the necessary film, lenses, and accessories before each occasion. Choose the best equipment for each situation on the basis of what you hope to show, how you wish to represent the subject, and of course the conditions under which you will be taking the photographs. For example, tabletop compositions at home may require seamless paper, a macro lens, a tripod, and lights. Informal environmental portraits outdoors are often best accomplished with a moderate telephoto lens, medium-speed film, and perhaps a reflector to fill in shadows. Here are some typical situations and subjects, with practical techniques for tailoring equipment and style to each.

You should plan out your photographic requirements and equipment in advance, especially when shooting on location. Lights, reflectors, tripod, cable release and a wide-angle lens were necessary for this shot. Despite their deceptively simple appearance, set-up shots call for attention to a great number of little things that spell the difference between success and failure. Photo: B. Krist.

Use the most effective focal length lens for the kind of portrait you want to create. Full figure and ¾ length portraits can be made with normal (50-55mm) lenses. To avoid distortions, head-and-shoulder portraits usually require the use of a longer lens (75-135mm). Photo: K. Tweedy-Holmes.

Portraits

Choose a moderate telephoto lens for close head-and-shoulders compositions. On a 35mm camera a lens between 70 and 135mm, is excellent
because it delivers a pleasing perspective without making noses, heads,
ears unusually large in the photograph. A normal 50mm lens used close
enough to fill the frame with only a head and shoulders is likely to render
the closest features too large.

For full-length figures a normal 50mm lens is ideal. The angle of view
permits you to fill the frame with a full figure without moving too far back.
A moderate telephoto lens may be useful for full figure compositions outdoors, but in most rooms you won't be able to get far enough away to take
in the full subject. At the other extreme a wide-angle lens, perhaps the
28mm, offers so wide a view that a single full figure will be too small in the
frame.

Groups of people, especially indoors, are easily photographed with a
moderate wide-angle lens such as the 35mm. With any wide-angle group
portraits keep your subjects away from the extreme edges of the frame,
since wide-angle optics show edge lines as curves, making people at the
edge look deformed. On the other hand, you can use this lens characteristic
creatively, to emphasize some feature. For example put the arms of a body
builder closest to the lens to make the muscles look bigger. To glamourize a
flowing dress, photgraph the model from a low angle with a moderate
wide-angle lens.

Portrait Poses. Pose your subjects to fit the mood. Distinguished in-
dividuals, especially older people, may look best in a formal setting with
conservative clothing, perhaps in a three-quarter pose. Have them sit in a
comfortable chair or stand behind a chair on which they can place their
hands. Position the subject's body in profile to the camera, with the face
turned toward the camera. Leaning slightly toward the camera will make
the person look more friendly, while looking down toward the camera
gives an aloof look, as does a low camera angle.

Coach your subjects to wear attractive clothing that complements
their personalities. Extreme contrasts of color are difficult to light and
print successfully. Avoid white clothing or dense black. People with
distracting skin blemishes may want to use a thin coating of pancake
makeup to cover up flaws before the photographs are taken. Take a few
minutes to be sure hair and clothing are neatly and attractively arranged
before taking exposures.

Children look best when given something to do. Let the child play with
a favorite toy or perhaps eat a snack as you take the photographs. Outdoors, children are fun to photograph informally, running around the
garden, playing games, or just sitting in a quiet place looking at a flower.
Most portraits of people are pleasant when taken at the subject's level,
with the lens pointing at the head. Beware of using high camera angles on
children since that perspective may make them look like dwarfs.

Panning is a good way to capture fast action when you don't have quite enough light for an action-stopping shutter speed. Follow the subject with your camera as it moves across the picture area, keeping the subject properly located in the finder. At the desired moment, press the shutter release while continuing to move the camera. Photo: H. Hoefer/APA Productions.

Sports and Fast Action

Capturing fast action requires a rapid shutter speed if you want crisp detail in the subjects. Moderate to slow shutter speeds render moving subjects in various degrees of blur. The larger the subject is in your frame the faster the shutter must be to freeze action. Also, subjects moving *across* the frame need a faster shutter to stop their action than subjects moving directly toward or away from the camera. With a few practice rolls you will learn how fast a shutter speed you need to stop various types of action.

Panning. A useful technique for showing moving subjects sharply at moderate shutter speeds involves panning the camera, or following the subject as it moves across the camera's field of view. To photograph a racing car at 1/125 or 1/250 sec., start panning your camera while the car is off to one side of the area. Keep moving (panning) the camera to keep the car in the same position of your finder. When the car reaches the point you want to capture, *continue moving* with the action as you release the shutter. This technique usually creates a great sense of speed in the picture because it shows the background as a blur but captures the moving subject sharply.

Lens-Selection. Lens selection for sports and fast action depends on how close you can get to the subject. If you are photographing skaters from their level, on the floor or ice, a moderate wide-angle or normal lens is useful. For spectator sports where you are confined to the sidelines choose a telephoto lens.

Zoom telephoto lenses, in the 80–210mm range, are useful for baseball, football, soccer, and other sports where you have to follow action that moves close, then far away. The more you know about a sport or fast-moving activity such as dancing or bullfighting, the better your action photography will be.

Pre-Focusing. When action is moving fast you may only have time to compose and release the shutter. Pre-focus your lens on a specific place in the field of action, then follow the players with panning and perhaps (if you have the lens for it) zooming. When the players get to the site of pre-focus, take the picture. Photographers who specialize in capturing fast action or sports often use a motor drive to advance the film rapidly. A camera with telephoto zoom lens, motor drive, and trigger release frees you to follow action and focus. Remember to select a fast film (ISO/ASA 100 or more) so you have a choice of motion-stopping shutter speeds with useful f-stops.

Here, the photographer waited for the moment of "peak extension"—the diver appeared almost still for a fraction of a second before beginning his descent. A fast shutter speed and good timing ensured the success of this picture. Photo: J. Peppler.

Landscapes and Buildings

Landscapes and architectural subjects require similar treatment when they are photographed as part of scenic views. Showing broad areas of landscape, sky, sea, or buildings requires careful composition. Fill the frame with meaningful material; experiment with placing foliage, an arch, or a branch against the sky. Decide if you want to feature the sky (as in a sunset) or the land (as with a field of grain). Avoid placing equal portions of land and sky in the frame.

Search for graceful patterns within the composition. A path or stream provides more interest when it runs diagonally through the picture than vertically or horizontally. A building may take on a more dramatic appearance if you use a nearby statue or winding path to lead a viewer's eye toward your main subject. An S-shaped curve through the frame is usually attractive and can often be found if you do some searching. A river or flowerbed becomes a dramatic picture when graceful curves are captured on film.

Architectural Subjects. Some buildings look best when seen from one side, from a corner, or framed within a garden arch, tree branches, or part of another nearby structure. On the other hand, buildings designed along very symmetrical lines, such as seventeenth- and eighteenth-century palaces, Greek and Roman temples, medieval churches, and many modern public buildings, are meant to be viewed from a specific angle—usually from the main entrance in a direct, straight-on view. In these cases, take a few frames of the building from this angle, with a composition that balances the structure perfectly. Then, for interesting variations, explore low-angle views and close-ups of building details. In a photo display or slide program these varying studies of the same structure will help to capture interest. A technique from motion-picture work is useful: begin with a wide view, then move in for a medium shot, and finally add interest by using your telephoto lens for detailed close-ups.

Tall Buildings. Pointing a camera up at a tall building causes the straight lines to converge, making the tall subject appear to be leaning back. To avoid this odd, tilted-back effect, try to find a vantage point from the upper floors of a nearby building or higher ground, then point the camera directly at the subject. You will probably need a wide-angle lens to encompass all or most of your subject.

Framing your architectural subject with part of another building or structure can add a sense of scale and depth. Photo: R. Holle.

Close-up photography need not be an expensive proposition. A couple of screw-in supplementary lenses can be added to your SLR kit for occassional close-ups. For frequent close-focusing endeavors consider getting a macro-focusing lens, which provides optimum results. Photo: C. M. Fitch.

Close-up Views of Small Subjects

Creating dramatic close-ups of small, nearby subjects is quite simple with modern 35mm SLR cameras. The single-lens reflex design permits you to get exact composition, preview depth of field, check focus, and use different lenses. However, because most normal 50mm lenses focus only to about two feet, which is not close enough to fill the frame with a really small subject, you must use some type of close-focusing attachment.

The Inexpensive Approach. The least expensive way to focus closer is with clear screw-in close-up, or supplementary lenses that fit directly on your normal camera lenses. These screw-in close-up lenses look like clear filters and come in all the popular accessory sizes such as 49mm, 52mm, and 55mm. Try to buy the correct size for your equipment; while adapter rings (to fit mismatched sizes to your lenses) are available, these may darken the corners of your images and are one more thing to buy. Well-stocked photo stores can offer you the screw-in size to fit your lens correctly.

Lenses of various powers can be combined. For example, to get a +3 effect, screw in a +2 lens, then a +1 lens. (Always put the most powerful close-up lens closest to the camera.)

Printed tables usually come with these inexpensive lenses, showing you how much area is covered. The lowest-power close-up lenses are numbered +0 or +1. As the numbers go up (+3, +4, +5, etc.), the power increases and the lens will focus closer. Using more than two close-up attachments together is not a good idea because sharpness suffers and you are likely to get corner darkening (vignetting). Also remember that because depth of field is very shallow when you focus close, you must use small f-stops (f/11 or smaller) to get the sharpest results.

A telephoto lens can render sharp results when fitted with a weak close-up lens such as a +0 or what some manufacturers offer as +¼ or +½. The stronger supplementary lenses (+1 through +10) are best suited to normal 50mm optics, but in all cases use the smallest f-stop possible; otherwise sharpness, especially at the edges, will decline.

With a constant light source such as photoflood lamps or the sun, most through-the-lens camera meters will read correctly. However, some cameras require a stop-down metering technique if the lens is separated from the camera body by an extension of any kind. This means you must close down the iris manually to a given f-stop in order to get an accurate meter reading. Check your camera instruction book for detailed metering instructions.

Extension Rings. Extension rings (or longer tubes) that go between the camera lens and the camera body permit your lens to focus closer than normal because they move the lens away from the film plane. These extensions preserve the sharpness of your image better than the less expensive screw-in close-up lenses. However, as your lens is moved away from the film the light is reduced; therefore, extensions require exposure compensation if your camera does not have a through-the-lens meter.

Macro Focusing. Lenses that are designed to focus very close, called macro-focusing lenses, are the most versatile to use. If you enjoy doing close-up photography, a macro lens is an ideal choice. The macro lens will give greater sharpness and versatility than screw-in close-up devices. With a macro lens you can focus on distant objects, medium distances, or very close. While the macros are designed to yield maximum sharpness at close distances, the modern types are perfectly suited to general photography as well. With a short extension tube many macro lenses will produce a life-size subject on film.

A bellows is seldom required for moderate close-ups. But if you are interested in doing extensive photography of objects smaller than your negative size, a bellows unit will be more flexible than fixed-length rings and tubes.

Bellows. For larger-than-life-size close-ups, a bellows is useful. The bellows attaches between the camera and the lens to provide continuously variable extension. The further you extend the bellows, the closer you can focus.

Lighting Close-Ups. Lighting small subjects requires greater precision but less equipment than larger subjects. With natural light, use the sun

If you are using electronic flash, it may be difficult to predict how the light will look and where reflections will occur. If your flash equipment does not have a focusing/model light, you can get a general idea of what the final image will look like by holding a small reflector spot bulb (available in electrical and hardware stores) in the same position as the flash. This improvised focusing light will permit you to make adjustments in general lighting effects. Double-check that shadows are where you want them and that any distracting reflections are eliminated.

If you must have the subject three inches or less from the lens, use a circular electronic flash unit called a ringlight. When a subject is very close to the lens it is difficult to aim adequate lighting where you need it. The circular ringlight screws directly onto the lens and gives a flat, even light. If the pictures look too flat for your taste, combine the ringlight with direct flash held off to one side or high behind the subject, or cover part of the ringlight tube.

Coins and other textured or engraved objects will show markings best if you skim sidelight across the surface, while flat subjects such as stamps look best with even frontlighting. Highly reflective surfaces like silver may have so many highlights that the picture is unattractive. Reduce reflections by diffusing the flash through a tent or dome of white tracing paper, thin cloth, or photographic diffusion material, and insert the camera lens through a slit in one side.

Indoors, suit the light source to the subject. Still-life compositions of non-perishable objects (jewelry, ceramics, coins, etc.) can be well lighted with photofloods or quartz lamps. More perishable objects such as foliage, flowers, or food may wilt from the hot, continuously burning lamps, so the short bursts of electronic flash may be the best.

To properly bring out the texture of your subject, you will have to arrange the lighting appropriately. Fabrics and rough surfaces are best lighted from the side. On the other hand, to produce even, flat lighting for smooth surfaces, paper, and similar items, place the light at the camera or otherwise head-on.

Casting sidelight across the surface of textured and engraved objects will show their various markings to best advantage. Photo: L. Jones.

Special Effects

Planning for special effects is an exciting part of photography. Whether created in the camera or in the darkroom special effects are a challenge to your imagination.

Double Exposures. Certain special effects need only manipulation of your usual camera and lens. For example, many cameras permit precise double exposures. Read your instruction book to see if the shutter can be reset for a double exposure without moving the film. If your camera does not have such a capability, see the Technique Tip below.

Remember that when a double exposure is made, the film is exposed twice. Therefore, the two images must each receive only about half their normal exposure to achieve correct overall exposure.

Prisms. Clear single- and multiple-prism lens attachments are fun to use. A favorite type has prism ridges on one half and plain glass on the other. The repeat image effect looks like rapid-fire electronic flash was used to capture multiple exposures on a single frame.

Color Effects. Several filters are available that create a rainbowlike effect from any direct reflection of light within the image. Such diffraction filters are called Colorburst, Rayburst, Rainbow, and similar descriptive names by their manufacturers. They are exciting devices for showing extra color in the sky, water, or in photographs of buildings where the sun reflected in a window can be turned into a burst of multicolored light. These diffraction-type filters need no increase in exposure.

Technique Tip: Making a Double Exposure

With cameras that do not have a special button or slide-switch for double exposures, but that do have a push-in rewind button, you can often get good results by following these steps:

1. Take the first exposure.
2. Push in the rewind button on the camera.
3. Hold the rewind knob tightly so the film cannot move.
4. Cock the shutter by operating the film advance lever.
5. Take the second exposure.
6. Advance the film for the next normal photograph.

If your camera does not hold the film completely still with this procedure, you may want to fire off one blank frame (put the lens cap on) after each double exposure is made. This will prevent an unintentional overlap with the following frame.

Double exposure can be done with many cameras that have a special provision for it. Others with a push-in rewind button can often be used as well. Remember to give half the normal exposure for each image used in a double exposure. Photo: M. & C. Werner.

Combined Movement and Stop-Action with Flash. A striking effect can be obtained by photographing a moving subject at a slow shutter speed under available light combined with electronic flash. The result is a sharp, frozen image plus a moving color blur on the same frame. A tripod and a shutter-release cable are necessary to achieve this effect, which is done as follows:

1. Focus and compose the photograph.
2. Select a slow shutter speed, perhaps ½-sec.
3. Set the lens opening for the correct *f*-stop according to the meter suggestion, using available light. If there is not enough available light, arrange a spotlight, photoflood, or other constant light source. If the meter still will not give a usable *f*-stop at the slow shutter speed, you must use a faster film or increase the light intensity.
4. Set your electronic flash to give an exposure within one *f*-stop of the available light exposure. For example, if you are taking the photograph at ½-sec. at *f*/5.6, use the flash at a distance and power that gives a correct exposure between *f*/8 and *f*/5.6.
5. Take the exposure as the subject is moving.

The long exposure will show a moving subject while the short burst of electronic flash will stop the subject, giving a sharp image.

High key effects emphasize light tones and impart a sense of delicacy that is excellent for portraits of young women. Use soft main lighting and plenty of unobtrusive fill light with full exposure (or even slight overexposure). Photo: R. Farber.

High-Key and Low-Key Effects

When a photograph contains a combination of delicate light tones, from pure white to the middle grays but with no true blacks or dark heavy colors, it is called a high-key effect. The other extreme, a combination of dark, somber tones with no true, sparkling white, is called a low-key effect. Both of these variations from the usual full range of tones can be used to create moods in your photographs.

The high-key effect is appropriate with winter landscapes, children, young women with backlit hair against a beach or sky, or flowers in delicate pastel colors. A combination of high-key lighting with a soft filter is a good way to hide wrinkles and other skin blemishes in portraiture. The soft filter smooths out the image, making everything seem slightly soft yet not so fuzzy that the personality is lost. Soft filters come in various strengths, with a No. 1 being the least soft and becoming progressively softer as the numbers increase. Indoors, soft, diffuse lighting can be obtained through the use of umbrella reflectors.

Low-key effects are appropriate for studies of bark, woodlands, somber city views, and situations where you wish to create a sad, oppressive, or mysterious mood. Low-key lighting is generally directional, in contrast to the diffuse high-key style. When you are creating a low-key image, select an environment with dark colors and have models wear black or dark tones. Meter from the light tones to render them slightly darker in the final photograph.

Low-key effects emphasize a dark, moody viewpoint. Slight underexposure or predominantly dark-colored subjects can add a touch of mystery to the scene. Photo: B. Docktor.

Index